STUGOTZ'S PERSONAL RECORD BOOK

STUGOTZ'S PERSONAL RECORD BOOK

The REAL WINNERS and LOSERS in SPORTS

JON "STUGOTZ" WEINER
and DAN STANCZYK

RANDOM HOUSE
NEW YORK

Published in the United States by Random House,
an imprint and division of Penguin Random House LLC, New York.

Random House and the House colophon are
registered trademarks of Penguin Random House LLC.

Drawings by Angel Resto

Hardback ISBN 978-0-593-73408-7
Signed ISBN 978-0-593-97763-7
Ebook ISBN 978-0-593-73410-0

Printed in the United States of America on acid-free paper

randomhousebooks.com

2 4 6 8 9 7 5 3 1

ScoutAutomatedPrintCode

FIRST EDITION

To my mom, whom we lost nearly four years ago but whose presence I feel every single day. Thank you for always encouraging me, teaching me, inspiring me, and pushing me well past my boundaries. Your unwavering belief in me is what gave me the strength and confidence to get behind a microphone, stand in front of a television camera, and, yes, write a book. I wrote a book, Mom. I love you and miss you so much.

—Stugotz

To my parents,
for always encouraging me to write.

—D. S.

FOREWORD
by DAN LE BATARD

BEFORE WE EMBARK ON THIS ABSURD JOURNEY, LET ME tell you a little bit about the author and his history. He grew up in New York. Played lacrosse. Went to a small Northeast college. He has two decades of experience in the sports-radio business, much of it at ESPN. He seems to know everyone in our industry, and he leveraged every one of those relationships to somehow get this project made. He started *STUpodity* and created Weekend Observations. But that's enough about Dan Stanczyk.

The star of our story, and the start of our story, is the mighty Stugotz, who court-jestered his way up the sports-media ladder in a way never before seen. Yes, he owes an eternal debt on this project to his producer, Stanczyk, and that debt, like all of Stugotz's others, will remain forever unpaid. But I can make the argument that, in the history of books, in the history of words, a published work has never quite been written like this, with heavy lifting farmed out to Stugotz's famous industry friends in the most boorish of fashions (more on that in a moment). Stugotz deserves all the credit for being the unprecedented kind of shameless required to make something this shamelessly loud and unique.

This book is a shining monument to Stugotz's illustrious career and his ultimate dream scenario—everyone else does the work and he collects the royalties. This is what it is like to love Stugotz. All the opinions in this book are indeed his, but I would bet big money that I've already typed more words for this book in three paragraphs than he has in three years.

This all started, as so much genius does, with profound laziness burped out on the radio. Stugotz stubbornly refused to give credit to Kevin Durant for winning a championship after joining a Golden State Warriors team that was already great without him. It was a throwaway line. Stugotz said that Durant would never have a championship in his personal record book, even though he has two in the empirical ones that matter a lot more than this one.

We mocked him for this, of course, saying that record books are just a documentation of factual history and that you couldn't just make up your own personal record book to usurp the truth whenever you wanted. How wrong we were. It is such an alpha move, not only publishing this proof that we were forever wrong but *also* making us all write words in it for free. We initially laughed at him. Now he laughs at us. Stugotz, unlike Durant, always wins.

There has never been a sports media member quite like him, so honest about his lying, so committed to a lack of commitment, so inconsistent about consistency. You aren't supposed to be able to climb to the very top of any business that way . . . except for maybe President of the United States. But through a combination of charisma and magic, this tiny giant has planted his flag at the top of the sports mountain. Stugotz's phlegm-soaked howls have echoed from coast to coast and beyond, taking championships away from Durant, crushing LaMarcus Aldridge for blowing a game he won, and blasting Andy Reid for having the audacity to choose Patrick Mahomes over Alex Smith . . . all while starting one season of football betting a remarkable 0–17. It is hard for something to be so wrong while feeling so right. But you know how he gets away with it? Because sports fans hear themselves in his emotional rants and ping-ponging opinions. His is the voice of the Everyman and Everyfan. And it has always stood out amid the starched expertise of the sportscoats opining on sports television as if they're better than him or you. Bold. Unafraid. Bravely and loudly wrong. This book is a testament to his eternal swagger, which looks like a waddle when he walks but sounds like a tornado when he talks. You can have your facts and your history books and your alleged memories of things you think you saw with your own eyes. He'll counter it with balls and dare you to tell him that he is wrong and ignore you when you do. He'll spit a bunch of inaccurate gibberish at you, tell you to look it up, and by the time you have done that, he is in another room counting his money.

His is one of the greatest magic acts in the history of our business. For twenty years, I've watched him trick everyone else into believing that *he's* the fool in this relationship. I've spent so much time laughing at his side, laughing at him, laughing with him, without ever realizing that he's laughing louder at me. You know how I know that I'm the biggest fool in our relationship? The mirror told me. I'm Patient Zero.

In my heart, I know I'm more than just an enabler for this Frankenstugotz monster that our show has grown and unleashed upon the world. I am his accomplice and getaway driver, which is why it feels like the authorities are closing in on me as I type this. I can already see myself standing guilty in front of a judge, not understanding exactly how we got here but somehow having the distinct memory of robbing a bank while standing next to a court jester . . . a court jester who somehow got away clean despite convincing me to threaten the teller while he stood next to me shooting his sausage-finger guns before running off with all the money and my freedom.

I have felt this way throughout most of our twenty years of marriage. But I've rarely felt it more than in being asked to write this foreword. Actually, as with many Stugotz adventures, even this isn't accurate or ethical. I wasn't *asked* to do this at all. I was told I was doing it. Via text. One with many misspellings. Including calling this a "forward." You know, like Durant. I wish I was creative enough to make this up. I am not. He told me it should be the honor of a lifetime to write this for him, for free, even though he requested an appearance fee to come to my wedding and then showed up late and in sneakers, changed his stink shirt in his car, and was spotted by my bride's most beloved guests *brushing his teeth* outside next door. Stugotz, God curse him, didn't even have the courtesy to tell me to write this "forward" in person, even though he sits next to me every day.

And, believe it or not, I have it better than some of the other people he bamboozled into this thing. Many of his friends and co-workers were told by email from people "representing" Stugotz that they had a deadline to submit their work . . . work they had no idea they were doing at all, never mind for free, until they got that emailed deadline from total strangers. I know this because so many of them called and asked me if any of this could possibly be for real. I assured them that it was. I had to patiently explain again and again that Random House was a very respected publisher, and that this was not just being printed at some random house.

By the way, I wasn't even Stugotz's first choice to write this "forward." First, he asked me without explanation for the telephone number of *Pardon the Interruption*'s Michael Wilbon, his sworn enemy. Then, when he didn't get an answer after what I'm sure was a shameless bombardment, he slinked back to me . . . and asked me to make the request of the more famous Wilbon myself, even though Wilbon truly hates Stugotz. After too much prodding by me, Wilbon said that he would consider it. But he didn't. He just ghosted me. So it isn't just that I'm doing this for free. The cost may be a friendship with Wilbon I've had for thirty years.

You'd think that I'd be a fairly obvious first choice because he has worked with me for two decades, our listeners will make this a bestseller, and most of the famous people contributing to this book for him are people he knows only because of our show. Hell, I'm pretty sure that he met Andre Dawson at my wedding, and that the only other time he ever spoke to him was when he called the confused baseball Hall of Famer recently and told him to write a rebuttal to Stugotz's argument that Dawson shouldn't have won Most Valuable Player in 1987. Dawson is a man so proud that when baseball's owners colluded against him as a free agent, Dawson told the Chicago Cubs to just pay him whatever they wanted in a blank contract . . . and then went out and won that MVP. I shudder to think how that call with my proud friend went. And am completely unsurprised that Stugotz somehow got him to agree. He's got a mysterious charm that way. And by mysterious charm, I mean the kind that brings people to their knees upon entering a just-used public beach bathroom that hasn't been cleaned for two months by striking government workers.

So Stugotz settled on me doing this instead. It has to be the single worst way that anyone has ever been assigned a "forward." It's also par for this particular "coarse."

I think there's the distinct possibility that he doesn't publish any of what I've written and just slaps my name on something that simply reads "Stugotz is the greatest," thinking that a foreword is supposed to be four words.

I tried doing all this as lazily as he would. With the artificial intelligence of ChatGPT. But the results weren't nearly good enough. Stugotz's future in this business seems to be a lot more secure than mine because none of the robots know how to create artificial stupidity.

True story: In the earliest incarnations of our radio show, a man who would revolutionize sports television came down to see if he could turn us into something televised. At the time, Stugotz was on air talking to the legendary running back Jim Brown about the size of his penis and how he had posed in *Playgirl* to make an ex-girlfriend jealous (Jim Brown did this, not Stugotz). The executive packed up his stuff rather immediately and told us that he couldn't do business with us. But not before pulling me aside in the hallway after watching Stugotz scheme in the commercial breaks and saying in a shocked stupor, "Oh, my, GOD, I thought he was just playing a character. I can't believe that this person is real."

I'm pretty certain that Stugotz hasn't read this, even though I sent it to him months ago. All he told me about it by way of feedback was that it was "long."

If you have come this far in the journey, it means that you are likely a member of one of the most loyal audiences in the history of sports media. A cult, some might say. Which makes this a bit of a religious text. Which means that you know just how much of a miracle it is that it ever got made. But after lending Stugotz what little credibility I have left that he hasn't destroyed, I can make you this promise about the adventure ahead:

He found the right people and the write people to take advantage of, the ones who love him, the ones who take more pride in their work than he does, so that reading this will feel even less like work than writing it was for him.

CONTENTS

STUGOTZ'S PERSONAL RECORD BOOK

1

NO GUTS, NO GLORY

CLOSE YOUR EYES FOR A MINUTE. GO BACK TO THE LATE 1980s when the Chicago Bulls, led by Michael Jordan, couldn't get past the Detroit Pistons. They were so close, losing in six games in 1989 and in seven games in 1990, but they just couldn't get past them. You could see the devastation on their faces. You could feel their heartbreak. They knew how close they were.

Keep 'em closed. I know it's tough to do that and read this book at the same time, but you're going to have to find a way, because this won't be the last time I ask you to do this. Rather than come back and try again, imagine that Michael simply left the Bulls and joined the Pistons. I know, it's jarring. I'm sorry. I almost had to go to the hospital the first time I tried.

You can open your eyes. By now, you should know the story. Jordan used the losing as fuel. He stayed with the Bulls, worked even harder, and Chicago beat Detroit in the 1991 Eastern Conference Finals en route to the first of three straight championships. That's what basketball is all about. What sports is all about. What being a champion is all about. A little thing I like to call "The Climb." When you can't quite get to the mountaintop, you work even harder, add pieces, keep grinding, keep chopping, put the blinders on, come back and try again.

Unless, of course, you are Kevin Durant.

Let's fast-forward from Jordan's era to the 2016 Western Conference Finals. Kevin Durant was still playing for the Oklahoma City Thunder, Russell Westbrook was still his built-in excuse if anything went wrong, and they were up three games to one on the Golden State Warriors. One game away from the NBA Finals. So close to beating what many were calling one of the best teams of all time. The Thunder were on the precipice of the aforementioned mountaintop.

But Durant fell apart, shooting 22 of 63 combined from the field in Games 5 and 6, and Oklahoma City eventually lost to Golden State in the decisive seventh game. So close. Heartbreaking. All that work, all that sweat, the travel, the dedication, and they still came up short. And it's OK that KD wasn't great in those games. It happens. The Thunder wouldn't have been in that position without him. I get it. It's what happened next that makes it impossible for me to look past.

What you do in that situation, if you are one of the three best basketball players in the world and you are playing with another top ten player, is this: take a little break and then get back to work with your team. Like Jordan did. What you definitely *don't* do is leave the team that worked so hard with you and join the team that you couldn't beat.

Nope. Sorry.

You gagged. Not them. As one of the three best players in the world, it's your responsibility to come back and fight with the guys that you led. Yes, even if one of the guys is Dion Waiters. That's what the all-time greats do. They make champions out of guys like Dion Waiters. Dallas Cowboys legend Michael Irvin—The Playmaker—once told me there are two types of athletes: ones who put rings on other people's fingers and ones who allow others to put rings on their fingers.

Speaking of Dion Waiters, here are the Top 5 people in sports and entertainment who connote something you would find in a restaurant.

THE TOP 5 PEOPLE IN SPORTS AND ENTERTAINMENT WHO CONNOTE SOMETHING YOU WOULD FIND IN A RESTAURANT

OUTSIDE LOOKING IN (OLI)

Jerod Mayo
Clarence Weatherspoon
Phil Coke
Cris Dishman
Jarrod Saltalamacchia
Dion Waiters
Willie Glass
Stewart Cink

5. Dave "Soup" Campbell
4. Antrel Rolle

3. Dottie Pepper
2. Sauce Gardner
1. Manute Bol

Anyway, you know I'm right about this. It's impossible to disagree. Even KD knows he took a shortcut. Notice how sensitive he was when he was in Golden State? That was because he knew he cheated. He *knew.* And suggesting that one of the reasons he chose Golden State was to be close to Silicon Valley? No way. Silicon Valley would have come to Oklahoma City. Silicon Valley? What a joke. Here are the only reasons KD chose Golden State: Steph Curry. Klay Thompson. Draymond Green. And because he's gutless. OK, and maybe, just maybe, because he was sick of playing with Dion Waiters.

Champions don't leave their team before they become champions to join a team that is already champions—*especially* when those champions beat your team on the way to the Finals. KD took the easy path, plain and simple. And the easy path is never rewarded in my personal record book.

Do you know what the E in the Elias Sports Bureau stands for? Eleven, as in the number of players who have been named NBA Finals MVP multiple times, because Kevin Durant has no rings.

2

COUPLE OF GOATS CUTTING IT UP

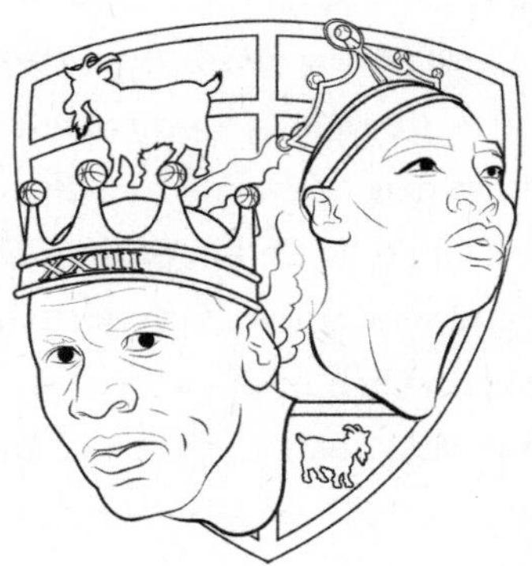

MICHAEL JORDAN IS THE GREATEST OF ALL TIME. THE GOAT. That is not an opinion. That is a fact. He made The Climb, conquered the Pistons, and went on to win three straight NBA Championships from 1991 to 1993.

On the heels of that third championship, when he was thirty and at the peak of his powers, he abruptly retired. Some say that he was embroiled in a gambling scandal that involved the Mafia and the league forced him to step away. Others say he wanted to try baseball while he was still young enough, because his father, who was murdered the summer before MJ retired, had always wanted him to. Jordan himself said that he lost the sense of motivation of having to prove himself because he had reached the pinnacle of his profession. But it was the gambling. I know an addictive personality when I see one.

Jordan's baseball career was largely forgettable. He batted a paltry .202, barely clearing the Mendoza Line, and hit just three home runs in 127 games for the AA Birmingham Barons and manager Terry Francona. Tito. The most memorable part of Jordan's baseball career was the way it ended—with a two-word announcement, which he faxed to reporters in March 1995, that read, "I'm back." I assume less than 10 percent of you reading this know what a fax is. It was the equivalent of getting an email, except the message arrived out of a machine on a piece of paper after about twenty-five seconds of loud noises.

Upon returning to the NBA, MJ and the Bulls picked up right where they left off and won three straight championships. Jordan's singular dominance was simply too much for the rest of the league to handle. In each of the six championship seasons, Jordan led the league in scoring and was named NBA Finals MVP.

Six for six. Every time Michael got to the Finals he won. You can't say the same for any of the other all-time greats. That's why he's the GOAT.

When it comes to that kind of greatness, Jordan has few peers. Wayne Gretzky is certainly among them. Muhammad Ali comes to mind, too. Tiger Woods is probably the closest comp. Neither Jordan nor Tiger have the most hardware in their respective sports, but both have a case for being the best, or at least the most dominant, of all time. Serena Williams is definitely in that class as well. She's the most dominant female athlete of all time, the female GOAT. The Nanny. In the late '90s, she burst onto the scene and torched everything and everyone in her path.

Serena beat five Grand Slam champions in a row to win the US Open in 1999 as an eighteen-year-old. In 2002, she missed the Australian Open with a knee injury, but went on to win the next four Slams in a row, and became the #1-ranked player in the world in the process.

The so-called Serena Slam cemented her place atop women's tennis, and she did not relinquish that crown until after giving birth to her daughter in September 2017. Hell, she even won a Grand Slam at the Australian Open in 2017 while pregnant. Her twenty-three Grand Slam singles titles are the most in the Open Era, which is the only era I care about, and, if you're honest, the only one you care about, too.

According to the Women's Tennis Association (WTA), Serena has been ranked #1 in the world on eight separate occasions and for a total of 319 weeks. According to me, she's been ranked #1 in the world since 2002.

The NBA did not feel the same to me when MJ was on his two-year baseball hiatus. Similarly, women's tennis never had the same luster when Serena missed a Grand Slam. Something is very off when the best of the best aren't around to defend their place on the top of their sport. One of my closest friends, Ric Flair—the Nature Boy—often said, "To be the best you have to beat the best." By that logic, if the best isn't beaten then the best is still the best. Also, I have no idea if Ric Flair considers me to be one of his closest friends.

So I'm sorry, Justine Henin, but the four Grand Slams you won when Serena was injured no longer count. Same goes for the two you won when Serena didn't play, Kim Clijsters. And let's be real here. You're 2–7 all time against her. If she'd been healthy you would have gone home with an L instead of a trophy. I'm even taking away the four Grand Slams that Serena missed while pregnant. If she won the Australian Open in 2017 in the early stages of her pregnancy then she would have beaten Jelena Ostapenko on the clay, Garbiñe Muguruza on the grass, Sloane

Stephens in New York, and Caroline Wozniacki Down Under. It might seem harsh to take away Wozniacki's lone Grand Slam, but former Houston Texans star J. J. Watt, whom she briefly dated, would never have gotten that close to a championship.

Speaking of Houston, the only reason we call Hakeem Olajuwon "The Dream" is because that's where his two titles are. Listen to me, the Rockets needed a 2–18 night from John Starks to beat the Knicks in Game 7 of the 1994 Finals. Two for 18. I could go 2 for 18 in an NBA game. The Knicks. What a joke. I hate them.

MJ and the Bulls sandwiched the two years where Houston thought they won a title with three-peats. And if MJ were around in '94 and '95 they would have eaten the Rockets for lunch. It would have been an eight-peat, which I have trademarked.

So in fact, that's what did happen. Jordan never played baseball. The Bulls won eight straight NBA titles. Starks never went 2 for 18 in Game 7 because he wasn't in Game 7. You're welcome, John. The Rockets have zero rings. Robert Horry—Big Shot Bob—now has only five, which feels right, and Kenny "The Jet" Smith doesn't have any. That means he never got the job at Turner and that job went to me. The show is called *Inside the NBA with Ernie Johnson, Charles Barkley, Shaquille O'Neal, and Stugotz.*

3

BILL JAMES, IT'S ALL YOUR FAULT

MY BROTHER AND I WENT TO A GRATEFUL DEAD SHOW AT THE Nassau Coliseum in the spring of '93. We were already baked when we ran into our buddy Mikey, who had grown up with us on Long Island. He was with his dad, and the four of us started talking. After a few minutes of mindless banter, I asked Mikey's dad where he worked. He rattled off three letters more fluidly than I have ever uttered a sentence on the air. You could sense his confidence. He was 100 percent sure that I would immediately recognize the acronym that he had just proudly stated. Except it was gibberish to me. I think he may have said "QTF." I just know I had no idea what he was talking about. The only letters that meant anything to me were LSD. Ten minutes later he was still going on and on about something, and my brother interjected and said, "Where did you say you work, again?" Again, he confidently said those three letters, and again I had no idea what to make of the consonant sandwich he had just spewed in my face.

My brother and I finally made our way to the floor and basked in the brilliance of Jerry Garcia, Bob Weir, and the rest of the band. It's a Top 5 Dead Show for me. They opened with "Help on the Way," followed it up with "Slipknot," and also played "Fire on the Mountain" and "Brown-Eyed Women." The encore was "Brokedown Palace," which is among my Top 5 Dead Songs.

On the way home I asked my brother where Mikey's dad worked and, like me, he didn't have a clue.

And *that's* how I feel watching sports these days. Fans, announcers, and media types are tossing acronyms around as if everyone knows what they're talking about. Just this week, I heard VORP, BABIP, and something called SIERA, which I thought was Russell Wilson's wife. Enough already. I'm serious. Let me enjoy watching the games without all these ridiculous stats being shoved down my throat.

As far as I'm concerned, Bill James ruined baseball. Sabermetrics. The name of your sports system shouldn't sound like something out of *Star Wars*. At that point you might as well dress up in a costume, go to the convention center, and see who can recite the ID number on the Starship Enterprise fastest.

What I'm saying is, deep stats are for irredeemable nerds. They don't matter.

Why aren't hits, runs, home runs, RBI, and batting average enough? I can see with my own eyes that Pete Alonso crushed one to the left field bleachers. I don't need to know the launch angle, the exit velocity, and the wRC+. Enough with the plus sign being tacked on to everything, by the way. OPS+, Paramount+, whatever the hell wRC+ is, Apple TV+. It's too much. Why am I paying $300 a month so that my wife can watch old episodes of *Friends*?

What was I talking about? Oh, that's right, made-up stats. My dear friend Greg Cote of the *Miami Herald* dropped a PECOTA on me the other day while talking about the Marlins. It is possible he was speaking Spanish—it gets confusing down here—but if a guy like Cote, who routinely yearns for the way things used to be back in his day, has succumbed to the so-called analytics revolution, we're doomed.

I stopped paying attention to baseball for two or three seasons, and all of a sudden there are FIPs and WHIPs and someone is undoing some ZiPs and the whole thing is starting to sound a little too kinky.

A few years ago, Le Batard tried to tell me how great of a pitching performance someone had because their "game score" was over 100. Game score? This isn't a video game where each player's performance is rated numerically. You know what a game score is? Pirates 4, Cubs 3. That's a game score.

In basketball we have field goal percentage, effective field goal percentage, and true shooting percentage? I know Inuits have fifty words for snow, and that's great, but we don't need three numbers when one does the trick. You want someone's true shooting percentage? Take their makes and divide it by their takes. Done.

And then there's "box plus minus," a term so awful it sounds like a typo. *And* there's an offensive box plus minus and defensive box plus minus? Is this the math portion of the SAT? Here's a new stat: it's called rings plus minus. You put all of Jordan's rings and all of LeBron's rings in a box and see who has more. It's Jordan plus two, by the way.

In football we have something called quarterback rating, which measures how good a QB is on a scale from 0 to 158.3. God, I wish I were making that up. That alone should have been the end of analytics. A perfect score is 158.3. You cannot know that and think I am wrong.

In 2011, ESPN invented a new stat to measure quarterbacks called QBR. Take a guess at what those letters stand for. They did use a scale from 0 to 100 to make things easier, but now whenever I see quarterback rating or QBR I don't know if it's the old one out of 158.3 or the new one out of 100. I prefer passing yards, touchdown passes, interceptions, completion percentage, and the eye test.

About a week after the Dead show, I was rifling through my wallet and came across a business card. People used to give them out like Solo Cups at a frat party back in the '90s. This particular business card belonged to Mikey's dad. He must have given it to me at the Dead show. He was a regional manager for UPS.

Mike Schur, an Emmy Award–winning television writer who created *Parks and Recreation, The Good Place,* and *Brooklyn Nine-Nine*

YEARS AGO, I MET STUGOTZ AND THE REST OF THE PIRATE Ship when I wrote a piece on *The Dan Le Batard Show with Stugotz* for *Slate* magazine. I wanted to figure out how the show worked, exactly—how it was possible that the same

radio program could be both ridiculous and serious, erudite and profane, trenchant and utterly meaningless. I spent the day with them, listening, interviewing, observing. The piece ended up being quite long, because, I felt, it took some time to understand the nuance and sophistication of what the show was attempting to do.

Then, a couple of months later, Stugotz called me with a question. He had been doing a long-running bit on the show where he would mention his "personal record book," the context usually being some variation of: "Kevin Durant had to join Steph Curry in order to win a title, so in my personal record book Durant doesn't actually have any rings." That kind of thing. The point of the call was to say that he now actually wanted to write his "personal record book," which I said I thought was a great idea. Until I realized that he wanted me to write it, and for him to take the credit for it, as well as, presumably, all the money.

I explained that I had a job already, writing and producing TV shows, which took up a good deal of my time, and gently attempted to make him understand that ghostwriting a sports book for a guy I just met was not super high on my list of priorities. He said, "OK, gotcha," and hung up and I never talked to him again.

Years went by. In late January 2024 I received an email that said *Stugotz's Personal Record Book* was actually being written. But the way it was going to work was that Stugotz would write some angry rant about something he deemed stupid about the modern world of sports and then there would be rebuttals from other folks who would point out how stupid the rant was, and also here is one of the chapters he wrote, and also could I write one of these rebuttals?, and also it should be five hundred words or so, and also we need it in two weeks.

It is now two weeks later, and I am sitting in my office at Universal Television. I begin shooting a new TV show for Netflix literally tomorrow. I am currently eating lunch and simultaneously writing this essay for Stugotz's book—for no money, I should add—and for the life of me I cannot figure out why. How does he get away with this? Why do all his friends help him dig his way out of the holes he digs for himself? How did I turn down a job that would've paid me very little money, yet five years later accept essentially the same exact job for zero money? How does Stugotz always win?

I guess what I'm saying is: my article for *Slate* all those years ago probably didn't have to be as long as it was, because the answer to all of my questions is basically: "The show works because Stugotz is a con artist and putting a con artist next to Dan Le Batard is funny."

Also, everything he said about analytics and statistics in the chapter you just read is stupid, and you should ignore all of it.

4

THOROUGHDEAD

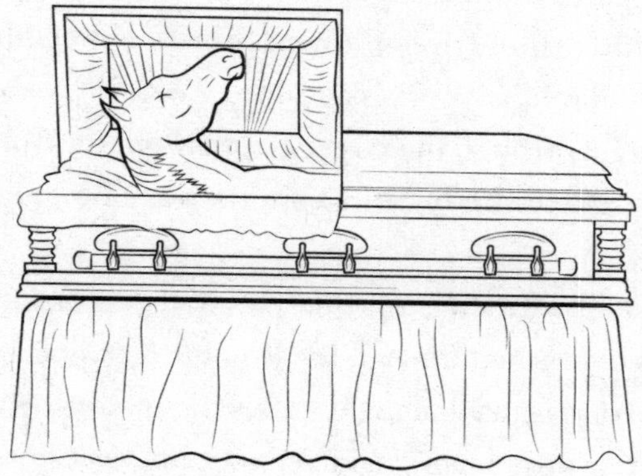

WHAT IF I TOLD YOU THAT THERE WAS A SPORT INFUSED WITH gambling and booze and fans only had to pay attention for three days a year? And that on those three days all the action took place in less than three minutes, which yes, sounds like Sunday nights with my wife, but fans have short attention spans, so that sport would be perfect, right? Wrong. That sport is horse racing and it's been dead since 2015.

Prior to 1950, the three most popular sports in America were boxing, baseball, and horse racing. Then pro football came around and soared past them all. Football was so dominant that even my Jets flew past the horses when Joe Namath guaranteed a win over the Colts in Super Bowl III. Broadway Joe.

Where was I? Right: baseball, boxing, and horse racing dominating the American sports scene. What a time that must have been. Baseball today is struggling to stay modern despite my efforts to add ponds to the outfield, boxing doesn't know what decade it is, and horse racing is dead. But between 1930 and 1950, all three were thriving, thanks in part to a string of dominance. Joe Louis was the heavyweight champion of the world for twelve years, the New York Yankees won seven World Series Championships, and seven different thoroughbreds captured the Triple Crown. Stories about those great champions filled the sports pages, led *First Take,* and helped Americans get through the Great Depression. As World War II ended, interest in the big three sports was booming. And so were babies.

The Boomers went on to have a good run as far as horse racing was concerned. In fact, horse culture had become so ingrained in Americana that in the 1960s there was a network television show whose main character was a talking horse. Think about that. A show, filmed in black-and-white, in which a horse spoke out loud to his owner. And it was a huge hit. *Mister Ed* lasted for six seasons.

The Boomers saw three Triple Crown winners in the 1970s. First, it was Secretariat in 1973, who somehow ranked #35 on ESPN's list of the greatest athletes of the twentieth century. A horse. Not a human. A horse. Please. The only animals on my list are a GOAT (Michael Jordan, #1) and an animal of nonspecific species (WWE Hall of Fame wrestler George "The Animal" Steele, #56, who, incidentally, is also in my Top 5 Teachers of All Time). The Boomers then witnessed Seattle Slew win it in 1977 and saw Affirmed complete the trifecta in 1978.

But things changed after that. History became harder to come by. First the Gen Xers and then the Millennials were left waiting for another horse to pull off a clean sweep of the Kentucky Derby, the Preakness, and the Belmont Stakes. With no horse to herald, the sport leaned into the pageantry and played up the pursuit of the elusive Triple Crown Trophy.

Each year the anticipation and the hope for the next Triple Crown winner grew. And grew. And grew. The only things that grew more in that time were Barry Bonds's head and Le Batard's waist size (couldn't help it, sorry). From 1997 to 2014 a horse won the first two legs of the Triple Crown only to come up short at the Belmont on nine separate occasions. You probably remember some of the names: Silver Charm ('97), Smarty Jones ('04), Big Brown ('08), California Chrome ('14). Those horses cost me a lot of hay.

That feeling of coming so close, though. That angst of another almost. The flirtation with history. It was all so intoxicating. Like tequila. And money.

Desire is a funny thing, too. Generally, getting what you wanted isn't as exciting as the wanting feeling you had in the first place. For example, when I was in my thirties and starting to make a name for myself in the sports talk radio game, I desperately wanted to move a little farther north. I yearned to be farther and farther away from Le Batard and the studio in South Beach. I needed to live on a golf course and in a gated community. My standing as a local celebrity simply demanded it.

That desire consumed me for over a year. I was looking at houses on Zillow all day during the show and haggling with real estate agents on the phone during the breaks. The mental energy I spent trying to find the perfect house was exhausting. It dominated my thoughts. Once I saw the house I'm sitting in right now, I knew I had to have it. There were a handful of other buyers that were interested, so I pulled out all the stops. It was like I was trying to get a brunch reservation on Mother's Day at a completely booked restaurant. Table for six. Prime time, baby. I'm talking celebrity name drops, leveraging my fame, and asking to speak with managers.

I was completely obsessed with owning the house up in Parkland. There was a bidding war and I was so locked into the pursuit and made so many bids that at one point I was bidding against myself. The day we moved in I was on top of the world, but the thrill of the purchase was short-lived. That burning feeling of desire was gone. I had a big house, but I had a bigger void where the wanting had been. After about a week, I started looking at houses even farther north.

It's a lot like fans of the Boston Red Sox prior to the fall of 2004. They love their baseball up in Boston, and every year they were reminded that they hadn't won the World Series since 1918. The championship drought grew year after year and it loomed over the franchise for decades. They had gotten so close, too. Game 7 in 1946. Game 7 in 1975. Bucky Fucking Dent in 1978. Aaron Fucking Boone in 2003. The closest, and most heart-wrenching of them all, though, came in 1986.

My father is a lifelong Sox fan. On October 25, 1986, he took me and my brother to Game 6 of the World Series at Shea Stadium. Boston led the Mets in the series, three games to two. My brother and I grew up on Long Island, so, like most of our friends, we were Mets fans.

Roger Clemens—The Rocket—pitched a gem for the Red Sox, but the Boston bullpen gave up a run in the bottom of the eighth and the game went into extra innings. In the top of the tenth the Red Sox scored two runs to take a 5–3 lead.

That was it. They were three outs away.

Wally Backman flew out to left to start the bottom of the tenth.

The Curse of the Bambino was about to be lifted. They were two outs away.

Keith Hernandez hit a ball to deep center for out number two.

It was actually happening. The Red Sox were about to win it all for the first time since 1918. They were one out away.

At that moment, my dad did what any Weiner man would do. He prematurely popped a bottle of champagne. Back then, you could bring just about anything into a stadium undetected. It was a different time. He'd tucked it inside his coat, hoping to celebrate the moment he had been waiting his entire sports fandom for.

Gary Carter singled to left. The Kid.

My father took a swig. Sure the Mets had a man on first, but the Red Sox were only one out away.

Pinch hitter Kevin Mitchell singled to center.

Another sip.

Strike one to Ray Knight, who had the second-best swing in his marriage. Two strikes away.

Strike two to Mr. Nancy Lopez. One strike away. The cork had already been popped, but the metaphorical one was about to explode.

Knight singled to center. The Kid scored from second. Mitchell moved to third.

Deep breaths. Long, deep sips. My father was still preening confidently on the outside, but internally he must have been a wreck.

Bob Stanley came in to face Mookie Wilson.

A wild pitch! Mitchell scored and the lead was gone. The banner that hadn't been put up yet was already down. Game 6 was deadlocked at 5–5.

Three pitches later, Mookie hit a dribbler to first and it went right through Bill Buckner's legs. Nancy Lopez's husband scored and we were on to Game 7 (which the Mets would win 8–5).

My brother and I ripped the champagne away from our father and in between swigs we poured it on top of our heads like we had just won the men's doubles championship at the Port Washington JCC. I was fourteen years old.

Buckner was a convenient fall guy, by the way. A patsy. I never quite understood why he got so much blame for Boston's loss. The game was already tied when that slow roller went through his legs. But then I looked up his stats from that series: 6 for 32 with one RBI? Fine, blame it on him.

The curse lingered year after year until Kevin Millar and the other idiots came back from being down three games to none in the American League Championship Series against the Yankees to win the title in 2004 (more on that series later). It was euphoric. Winning the World Series instantaneously unleashed all the emotions that had been pent up in the hearts and minds of Red Sox fans for generations. But after the parade, the ring ceremony, and the banner unveiling, it was over. A new season was at hand. Fans were still following the team, sure, but now they weren't hanging on every pitch. There was no way to replicate the eighty-six-year drought. And the Red Sox were good for a long time, too. They went on to win the World Series in 2007, 2013, and 2018, but I bet most fans can't tell you who they beat to win it all in 2007.

Prior to 2004, though, these same Red Sox fans had grown accustomed to heartbreak without feeling empty. Every April they believed that that year was going to be the year. They swallowed the pain. They internalized the suffering. They lived with both the hurt and the hope. It defined them. Knicks fans know what I'm talking about. But once you win . . . poof. Who are you now?

American horse racing fans felt like the cursed Sox fans in the '80s, '90s, '00s, and first half of the '10s. Except the feeling was more communal. There weren't thirty different fan bases in horse racing. There was just one. Everyone was in it together. Everyone rooting for the same thing. And every year, we were reminded of how long it had been since Affirmed won the Triple Crown in 1978. It seemed like every year a horse would win the Derby and the Preakness and we'd think that this year we'd finally get our Triple Crown winner. And every year we were let down. But that first Saturday in May the following year we'd be even more hopeful. More convinced that this year a horse would break through.

And then in 2015 it happened. American Pharoah won the Triple Crown, and the sport, which was elevated and supported by the desire of everyday Americans who wanted to witness (and wager on) history, instantly collapsed. Sportswriters could no longer write the piece about how long it had been and how this year would finally be the year for a Triple Crown winner. The industry could no longer gin up excitement in the pursuit of history. The chase was over. The thrill was gone. It was the rare double-double where a sport had its greatest day and also died at the same time.

Sure, the Kentucky Derby is still a spectacle, but it's a spectacle drenched in pageantry, decadence, and pomp and circumstance. Wealthy owners, private boxes, sundresses, stylish hats, Wes Welker handing out ecstasy pills (what?), mint juleps, the paddock (which isn't decadent at all, it's just a funny word), bloodlines, the bugle horn, "My Old Kentucky Home," and

Bob Baffert's luscious white hair. It's an excuse to get dressed up, have a cocktail or two, and wager on a race you know very little about.

Horse racing used to be part of the fabric of American sports. Now it's just glue.

Chris "The Bear" Fallica, formerly of ESPN's *College GameDay* and now with FOX Sports

ABOUT THE ONLY THING STUGOTZ HAS CORRECT HERE IS his ranking of George "The Animal" Steele, although the omission of "The Birdman" Koko B. Ware from the animal ranking list is a glaring one.

Did Stugotz forget 2018? I mean it's quite possible he was on the road with the Dead for a few months and it's all a blur. Justify was one of the biggest stories of the year. An undefeated colt won the Triple Crown.

American Pharoah winning the Triple Crown in 2015 not only didn't kill horse racing, it brought more buzz to the sport. Instead of wondering if the drought was going to end, it was "Who could win it this year?" And we didn't have to wait long for another Triple Crown winner, as it happened just three years later. The roar of Belmont Park that day in 2015 was a wall of sound. And the roar in 2018 was right there with it.

Don't give me any of this three-days-a-year garbage, either. Take a trip to Saratoga or Del Mar in the summer. Check out the San Gabriel Mountains in the backdrop at Santa Anita. Or the grounds at Keeneland. Those things are all annual rites of passage for not only the hardcore racing

community, but casual fans just looking for a great, memorable experience. How didn't you become captivated by the emotional story of Cody's Wish in 2023?

Oh, and, by the way, the thrilling 2024 Kentucky Derby just so happened to have the highest TV rating in twenty-five years and was the most wagered on Derby in history, so clearly there's no interest in horse racing.

Look, I get it. You're a beaten-down Jets fan like me. We have no hope. We're pessimistic by nature and the glass is usually about 35 percent full. You're from Long Island, so it's almost blasphemy to think horse racing is dead, as you basically grew up in the shadow of Belmont Park. You're just wrong here.

Happy to discuss further over lunch at White Castle and a day at the track.

The Rebuttal to the Rebuttal

Hey, Bear! I actually did forget about 2018. You know why? Because 2015 happened. You and Hank Goldberg cared, but fringe fans (the majority) like myself did not.

TOP 5 PEOPLE IN SPORTS AND ENTERTAINMENT WHO CONNOTE A BEAR

OLI

Bob Huggins
Brett Baier
Max Baer

5. Yogi Berra
4. Fozzy Whittaker
3. Pablo Sandoval, Kung Fu Panda
2. Tedy Bruschi
1. Pooh Richardson

5

THE [SEMI] FINALS

I HAD A FRIEND IN COLLEGE WHOM WE ALL CALLED THE BEAR. He was a much nicer Bear than Chris Fallica. The Bear I knew in college was a gargantuan creature with a grizzled beard from the outskirts of Chicago. He loved sports, gambling, tobacco, and alcohol, so we were close. The Bear had that slow, Midwestern way about him. He lumbered around campus and was friendly with everybody. If he owed you money, he would pay you back in thirty racks of beer.

The Bear was a fixture at parties and bars. One Friday early in my junior year, he asked me if I was going out later that night. I told him I was taking it easy because there was a huge party on Saturday and everyone was going to be there. Saturday's bash was something of a kickoff to the new school year. The Bear looked me dead in the eye and said, "You can't get to the Finals if you don't play the Semis."

You know what—and this is an odd statement—the Bear was right. Once I got back to the off-campus house I was living in with four other lacrosse players, I ripped three shots of Goldschläger and got ready to go. Sure enough, that night turned out to be one of my favorites from all of college. The line from the Bear stuck with me for the rest of my life. The night before a big event was no longer optional. There was no staying in. There was no taking it easy. Sure, sometimes I didn't make it to the kegger the next night or I was a shell of myself, but every once in a while the night before the huge party was ten times more fun.

"You can't get to the Finals if you don't play the Semis."

THE 1980 WINTER OLYMPICS in Lake Placid, New York, came at a time when political tensions were high between the United States and the USSR. The Cold War was near its peak. We hated them. They hated us. We were trying to promote democracy throughout the world. They were trying to promote communism. We were the Stephen A. Smith to their Skip Bayless. In December, the USSR invaded Afghanistan, a move that would eventually lead the United States and sixty-four other nations to boycott the 1980 Summer Olympics in Moscow.

The sanctions and embargoes placed on the Soviet Union in response to their invasion of Afghanistan were one thing, but we also nailed them where it mattered most: on the ice.

Not only had the USSR won the gold medal at the previous four Winter Olympics, they had utterly dominated. In Innsbruck ('64), Grenoble ('68), Sapporo ('72), and then Innsbruck again ('76), the Russians went 27–1–1 and outscored their opponents by a combined score of 175–44. The United States went 0–4 against them in that stretch and were outscored 28–7.

The Soviets dominated because they had grown men out there. You know how in Little League Baseball you sometimes see someone on the opposing team with a mustache and think, "There's no way that kid is twelve!" The Soviets were a team full of "twelve-year-olds" who had mustaches and beards and smelled like cheap vodka. The International Olympic Committee had an amateurs-only policy, but the Soviets were all trained professionals.

The United States skated into Lake Placid with the youngest team in the tournament as well as the youngest in the history of the U.S. national team. Coach Herb Brooks wanted talent and toughness. One component of the tryout was a three-hundred-question psychological exam. If you chose not to take it, you would not be considered for a spot on the team.

In the lead-up to the Winter Olympics, the United States played sixty-one exhibition games. In their final tune-up before heading to Lake Placid, they played the USSR in Madison Square Garden and lost 10–3. MSG hasn't been home to a winner in more than fifty years. The Knicks. I hate them. For their part, the Russians had gone 5–3–1 against NHL teams in exhibition games and even defeated the NHL All-Stars in a game, 6–0.

The United States and the USSR were rivals when it came to geopolitics, but when it came to hockey, the rivalry was more like the relationship between a hammer and a nail.

MEANWHILE, FOR NEARLY A century, the Boston Red Sox were the Washington Generals to the New York Yankees' Harlem Globetrotters. Decade after decade, the Yankees racked up American League pennants and World Series trophies while the Red Sox sputtered. New York represented the AL in the World Series thirty-nine times from 1920 to 2003 and won the World Series twenty-six times. In that same span, the Red Sox won the pennant just four times and failed to win a World Series. Boston routinely finished second to New York in the standings, including every year from 1998 to 2004.

The rivalry was every bit as bitter as it was one-sided. The Yankees just kept getting in the way of the Red Sox at the most pivotal stages. The Boston Massacre and Bucky Fucking Dent in 1978. The ALCS in '99. Aaron Fucking Boone in 2003. The Yankees were the dragon that the Red Sox could not slay.

STICK WITH ME HERE. Men's hockey at the 1980 Winter Olympics featured group play, where teams were split into two groups of six. Each team played the other five teams in their group. A win netted you two points. A tie earned you one point. And a loss got you no points. The top two teams in each group (based on points) then advanced to the medal round. Honestly, the whole setup feels like something out of European soccer and I'm going to do away with it real soon, don't worry.

Team USA tied Sweden, upset Czechoslovakia, and beat Norway, Romania, and West Germany to advance to the medal round. The USSR beat Japan, the Netherlands, Poland, Finland, and Canada by a combined score of 51–11 on their way to the medal round. Sweden and Finland also advanced and would face off, but the eyes of the world were on the game between the United States and the USSR.

. . .

IN 2004, THE YANKEES finished the regular season with the best record in the American League at 101–61 and won the AL East. They had Derek Jeter—The Captain, Alex Rodriguez—A-Rod, Gary Sheffield, Hideki Matsui, Mike Mussina—Moose, Orlando Hernández—El Duque, and Mariano Rivera—The Sandman. The Red Sox won ninety-eight games, second best in the AL, and clinched the wild card. Boston had Pedro Martinez, Curt Schilling, Manny Ramirez, David Ortiz—Big Papi, and Johnny Damon.

The two teams had been on a collision course all season. It had seemed destined that they would meet again in the postseason ever since Aaron Boone's walk-off home run in the bottom of the eleventh of Game 7 in the American League Championship Series the year before. Boston swept the Angels in the Division Series, and once New York took down the Twins in four, the ALCS rematch was set.

AS THE LATE HERB BROOKS famously said, "Great moments are born from great opportunity." And that's what Team USA had. That's what Team USA had earned. One game. If they played 'em ten times, the USSR might win nine. But not this game. The United States trailed 1–0, but five minutes later they equalized. They trailed 2–1, but in the waning seconds of the first period they took advantage of a Soviet mistake and tied the game at two. For some reason, the Soviet coach benched their all-world goalie after the first period, but the backup was no slouch. He didn't surrender a goal in the second period and the USSR scored on a power play to take the lead yet again. The United States went into the final frame down 3–2.

THE YANKEES WON GAME 1 of the ALCS behind the arm of a Moose, Mike Mussina. The Bronx Bombers took Game 2 as Jon Lieber outdueled Pedro Martinez, who gave up a two-run blast to John Olerud. Game 3 was a rout: Yankees 19, Red Sox 8. The Yankees were up 3–0 in the series and on the brink of another trip to the World Series. The Red Sox had their backs against the proverbial wall. No team had ever come back from a 3–0 series deficit. It had never happened.

THE AMERICANS WERE DOWN 1–0. They were down 2–1. And now they were down 3–2. They had twenty minutes to change the course of history. Nearly seven minutes into the final period, a Soviet went to the penalty box for high-sticking. The United States had mustered only two shots against the USSR's backup goalie, but now they had their chance. With the penalty ticking away, Mark Johnson slipped a shot into the net and the game was tied once again. Eighty-one seconds later, Mike Eruzione, the U.S. captain, blasted a shot from the high slot that found the back of the net. With ten minutes left to play, the score was United States 4, USSR 3. It was Team USA's first lead of the game.

GAME 4 OF THE 2004 ALCS was played in Fenway Park. The Yankees, leading the series three games to none, took a 4–3 lead into the home half of the ninth. New York's future Hall of Fame closer Mariano Rivera had just dispatched three straight Red Sox hitters to end the eighth inning and was looking for three more outs to send the Yankees back to the World Series. He was set to face the bottom of the Boston order. Kevin Millar, one of the team's self-described "Idiots" and the emotional leader of the Red Sox, led off the ninth and cowboyed up. He worked a walk and Dave Roberts replaced him as a pinch runner. Everyone in Fenway Park and everyone watching on TV knew that Roberts was going to try to swipe second base. He took off on the first pitch of the ensuing at bat and beat the throw from Yankees catcher Jorge Posada. Boston's third baseman Bill Mueller singled to center field and Roberts scored to tie the game at four. The game went to extras. Big Papi hit a walk-off home run in the twelfth and the Red Sox had lived to fight another day.

Ortiz delivered again in Game 5, singling home Johnny Damon in the bottom of the fourteenth inning to extend the series to a sixth game. Game 6. The bloody sock game. Curt Schilling had a torn tendon sheath in his right ankle. Blood seeped through his white sock throughout the game, turning the area next to his ankle a team-friendly red. Schilling grinded through seven innings, surrendering only one run, and the red sock led the Red Sox to a 4–2 win, which tied the series at three games apiece.

TEN MINUTES TO GO. United States 4, USSR 3. The Soviets hadn't lost a game at the Olympics in twelve years and they didn't want to start now, especially against their global enemy.

U.S. goaltender Jim Craig, in his Jason Voorhees mask, had to fend off a Soviet siege. Craig was blocking Soviet missiles left and right. With his blocker. With his stick. With his glove. One shot pinged off the right goalpost. The puck was flying all around the American zone. Herb Brooks wisely didn't fall into some prevent defense, though. The United States kept attacking, even getting some shots on net in the final ten minutes, but the crazed action was behind their own blue line. The Soviets had possession of the puck there with under a minute to go, but didn't pull their goalie. Craig kicked a shot away with thirty seconds to go. The puck was loose until Mark Johnson, who'd scored the game-tying goal, found it and passed it ahead. Team USA cleared the zone and the unthinkable was happening.

As Al Michaels famously narrated the final, improbable moments on ABC: "Eleven seconds, you've got ten seconds, the countdown going on right now! Morrow, up to Silk. Five seconds left in the game. Do you believe in miracles? YES!"

GAME 7. THE BEST two words in sports. All hands on deck. Win or go home. Before the game, the Red Sox watched the movie *Miracle* for motivation to complete the comeback. The Yankees had Bucky Dent throw out the first pitch. The Red Sox came out of the gate slugging. They knocked Yankees starter Kevin Brown around and led 6–0 halfway through the second inning. Johnny Damon hit his second home run of the game to put Boston in front 8–1 in the fourth, and the rout was on. The Red Sox won the game 10–3 and became the first team in MLB history to rally from a 3–0 deficit to win a postseason series. And they did it against their hated rival.

THE BEST TWO WORDS IN SPORTS

OLI

Penalty kicks
Butler Cabin
Buzzer beater
Deadline day
Magnolia Lane

5. Game 7
4. Amen Corner
3. Witching hour
2. Masters Sunday
1. "Hello, friends"

Think about the joy. The jubilation. The release of emotions after pulling off one of the greatest victories in the history of sports. Can you imagine if the U.S. hockey team had to play another game? Can you imagine if the Red Sox had to play another series? Me either.

Sometimes the Semis are actually the Finals. You know it when you see it. And those now count as the real rings.

So the Red Sox actually beat the Yankees to win the World Series. The United States beat the USSR for the gold medal. You can give the Russkies the silver. And the Finns can take the bronze on their way back to Helsinki. Speaking of Hell. Art Briles.

OH, AND WHILE WE'RE at it:

The Christian Laettner shot that beat Kentucky in the 1992 East Regional Final was actually for the National Championship.

The Seahawks' victory over the 49ers in the 2013 NFC Championship Game was actually Super Bowl XLVIII.

And the Manning–Brady showdown in the 2015 AFC Championship Game where the Broncos beat the Patriots 20–18 and the Pats missed on a two-point conversion with twelve seconds left was actually Super Bowl 50.

6

BUC YOU

WHAT CAME FIRST: THE CHICKEN OR THE EGG? THAT QUEStion was first asked by Plutarch a few thousand years ago, and it remained unanswered until 2021. The answer was neither the chicken nor the egg. It was the goat.

Tom Brady won six Super Bowls as the quarterback of the New England Patriots. More than any other player in NFL history. Throughout the 2010s, Brady was largely regarded as a possible answer in the "Who's the best quarterback of all time?" debate. Many argued for Joe Montana, John Elway, and Peyton Manning, whom Brady routinely drubbed throughout his career. Brady's excellence was not fully acknowledged, mainly because so many NFL writers and analysts thought he had the greatest coach of all time in Bill Belichick, guiding Brady from the sidelines.

For years the debate raged on. Who was more responsible for the Patriots' success: Brady or Belichick? Who had more of an impact on winning? The star quarterback? Or the mastermind coach?

That question is now stupid, because the answer is clear as day. Just beyond obvious. Asking that question is like asking, "What makes candy taste good: sugar or red dye?"

In Brady's first season away from New England, he won the Super Bowl with the Tampa Bay Buccaneers. What did Belichick and the Patriots do the year after Brady left? They went 7–9 and missed the playoffs.

We know that a great quarterback can cover up a lot of blemishes for teams, but was Brady also covering up for a lackluster coach the whole time he was in New England? Seriously. What has Belichick done without Brady to make you think he's one of the greatest coaches of all time?

Belichick was the head coach for the Cleveland Browns for five seasons and went 36–44. He made the playoffs once. Nobody would argue that's great.

After getting canned, Belichick ran to the arms of a truly great coach in Bill Parcells and hopped on board for stints with New England and the Jets. Belichick was even the head coach of the Jets for a day, which is probably when he lost any chance to be great.

After standing in the general vicinity of Parcells, The Big Tuna, Belichick was hired by the Patriots to be their head coach in 2000. He went 5–11 in his first season. Then Brady showed up and New England started winning, and winning big. They were the class of the NFL. Perhaps it was because Brady was a sixth-round pick and looked out of shape at the combine that people gave Belichick most of the credit.

In 2008, Tom Brady tore his ACL in Week 1 and was out for the season. And wouldn't you know it, the Patriots did not make the playoffs that year.

You could score a 0 out of 100 in pattern recognition and still be able to see what's happening here.

Belichick has never won a division title without Brady. Belichick has made it to the postseason twice in eleven seasons as a head coach without Brady. Belichick has won just a single, solitary playoff game without Brady. Herm Edwards has more playoff wins than Belichick does without Brady. And Herm won them with Chad Pennington.

But I'm supposed to believe that Belichick is the greatest coach of all time? Why? Where is the greatness without Brady? Seriously. He was a middling NFL coach who was gifted the single greatest quarterback of all time. Likely the greatest football player of all time. Possibly even the greatest athlete of all time. And the GOAT did what GOATs do. He won rings.

If Belichick is such a strategic genius, then wouldn't Brady have taken a step back without Belichick strategically masterminding everything from the sidelines? Wouldn't it have been difficult for Brady to adjust to a new head coach, a new scheme, and a new conference? Nope. He went out and won the Super Bowl in, literally, his *first year* away from the slovenly, monosyllabic, so-called genius.

With Brady, Belichick went 249–75. That's a 77 percent winning percentage. Without Brady he went 83–104. That's a 45 percent winning percentage. Marvin Lewis won 52 percent of his games coaching the Bengals. The *Bengals*. Wade Phillips won 56 percent of his games. So did Jason Garrett. My friend Adam Gase and his crazy eyes won 48 percent of his games with the Dolphins.

When the Patriots were winning Super Bowls, a bunch of Belichick assistants went on to get head coaching gigs elsewhere. They all flamed out pretty quickly: Josh McDaniels in Denver, Romeo Crennel with the Browns and Chiefs, Eric Mangini with the Jets and Browns, Matt Patricia with the Lions. The list goes on and on. For years, the explanation was that none of these assistants was the mastermind that Belichick was. I'm here to tell you that the Belichick coaching tree is littered with losers because Belichick isn't that good of a coach.

In ten years, it will be shocking that this whole Belichick or Brady thing was ever a debate. You know the saying "A rising tide lifts all boats"? That's what Brady was. The greatest tide in the history of tides. And now we've come to find out that Belichick was nothing more than an anchor that Brady dragged to six Super Bowl victories.

So, Belichick has to give Brady half of the rings he won with New England, giving Brady a total of ten and leaving Ol' Bill with five. He won two as the defensive coordinator of the Giants when he had Lawrence Taylor, the greatest defensive player in the history of the sport coming off the edge. Belichick is far from the greatest coach of all time. But by being in the right place at the right time and getting to coach LT and Brady, he is unquestionably the luckiest coach of all time.

7

SHAM SEASON

THE COVID-19 PANDEMIC OBVIOUSLY DISRUPTED SPORTS IN a major way. Games were canceled. Seasons were put on hold. Leagues scrambled to find ways to carry on. With no games to watch, most sports fans circled their calendars, tapped into their own nostalgia, and watched a ten-part documentary about the 1990s Chicago Bulls.

Millions upon millions of dollars were spent trying to figure out a way to play games as safely as possible. ESPN's Jay Williams thought the solution was cruise ships. That's right. At a time when passengers on cruise ships weren't allowed to disembark because some of them had tested positive for the novel coronavirus, Jay Williams thought cruise ships were the answer.

The NBA and its owners consulted with medical experts and created a bubble in Orlando to finish the league's season.

Major League Baseball and its owners consulted with their pockets and opted for a money grab.

The sixty-game regular season they decided on was a sham from the moment it was announced.

Sixty games? You cannot take a sport that has 162 games and condense it like that. You cannot lop off more than a hundred games and pretend like that's normal. You can't do it. I'll even concede that 162 is far too many. Reducing the number of games is part of my plan to fix baseball, a plan I work on every July and August while I'm waiting for football season to return. That said, anything less than a hundred baseball games does not count. Plain and simple.

Sixty games is basically a third of a normal season. That'd be like the NFL having a six-game season. The Jets still wouldn't make the playoffs in that scenario, but a six-game season would produce terrible results. With a full season you're allowed to have a bad start like the Patriots did back in 2014, go on to Cincinnati, right the ship, and go on to win a Super Bowl. I hate them.

Let's apply this logic to the NBA: it would be like their season being thirty games. Some players like Kyrie Irving and Kawhi Leonard might prefer a thirty-game season, but you can't do it, because it's ridiculous. The Heat started 9–8 in the first year of the Big Three and everyone was calling for Erik Spoelstra's job. They waltzed to the NBA Finals before losing to the Mavericks because LeBron was too scared to post up J. J. Barea. The best teams need time to separate from the pack. And speaking of the Mavs, in 2021 they started 16–18 and still ended up in the Western Conference Finals. Thirty games clearly isn't enough for a true NBA season.

The sixty-game season for Major League Baseball was such a joke that the Cardinals and the Tigers only played fifty-eight and nobody batted an eye.

The major benefit of a 162-game season is that the daily grind weeds out the pretenders, leaving only the best teams standing for the postseason. Typically, you don't even look at the standings until Memorial Day. Then the dog days of summer chew up all the teams and spit out the ones that have a chance to make it to the Fall Classic. It's a tried-and-true method.

Well, there was no weeding out in 2020. The weeds stayed in. And grew. Rob Manfred and company actually expanded the number of playoff teams from five in each league to eight. Think about that. In 2019, only a third of MLB teams made the playoffs. In 2020, more than half did.

Instead of getting the best teams in the postseason, in 2020 you got the Miami Marlins, a glorified Triple-A team. And you got the Astros and Brewers, who both lost more games than they won. That had never happened in the long, storied history of Major League Baseball. It was an embarrassing first, allowed only for the sake of the almighty dollar.

The watered-down playoffs didn't have quite the same buzz, either. The Division Series, the Championship Series, and the World Series were all held at neutral sites. No fans were allowed at the games. Part of winning the World Series is being down three games to two in the LCS and sending your ace to the bump on the road in front of seventy thousand screaming fans. That's playoff baseball. Pitchers getting out of big spots. Hitters poking the ball the other way in the clutch. The pressure. The tension in the ballpark that's almost tangible. All of that was eliminated in 2020. In 2020 you had losing teams out there kicking the ball around the infield. You had a bunch of kids on the Marlins who didn't belong anywhere near October baseball.

The money grab was one thing, but then Manfred and company just started making things up as they went along. Both leagues used the designated hitter (a good idea). Each half inning of extra-inning games started with a runner on second base (only in the regular season). Plus, after the season had already started, MLB reduced doubleheaders to seven innings apiece, even though a double dip of nine full innings had already taken place earlier in the season. Ernie Banks was rolling over in his grave. Mr. Cub said, "Let's play two." Not "Let's play one and a half." Manfred should be ashamed of himself.

I don't even know who MLB says won the World Series in 2020, because as far as I'm concerned it never happened. Sixty games. A watered-down playoffs. Rule changes on the fly. No fans. No road games. No season. No rings. Simple as that.

8

POINT FRAUD

I'M SICK AND TIRED OF STEPHEN A. SMITH, RYEN RUSSILLO, Amin Elhassan, Zach Lowe, Bill Simmons, and everyone else in the NBA analyst community telling me how great Chris Paul is. Enough. Yes, he ranks third in NBA history in assists, third in steals, and fifteenth in some stat the analytics nerds made up called PER (Player Efficiency Rating). I'm no exPERt, but his résumé still has a suPER glaring hole in it. These NBA types coddle CP3. Every year they crank up the excuse machine and hyperventilate over why it was someone else's fault that Chris Paul failed to win a title. Maybe he's not as amazing as they say he is?

Basketball is the team sport where one player can have the biggest influence. The best players take over games in crunch time. They put their teams on their backs and carry them to wins. They carry them to the playoffs. And they carry them to championships. And much like quarterback in football, point guard is the position of leadership. The best point guards settle their teams down during stressful situations. They rise above the pressure of the moment and get their teammates organized on offense. They orchestrate. They initiate. They penetrate. They create. And they don't consistently blow it in the playoffs.

So spare me this talk about how incredible Chris Paul is. He may be first all time in career assist-to-turnover ratio, but he's tied for last in the category that means the most: rings.

In 2008, Chris Paul led the Charlotte Hornets to the #2 seed in the Western Conference. They blew a 2–0 (and a 3–2) lead to the Spurs, culminating in a Game 7 loss on their home floor in the second round. Hopefully someone got CP3 a diaPER after pooping his pants in that series.

In his first year with the Los Angeles Clippers in 2012, the Spurs swept them in the second round. In 2013, they took a 2–0 lead on the Grizzlies in the first round before dropping four straight games by double digits. A total collapse.

In 2014, the Clippers not only gagged away a 101–88 lead with four minutes to play in a pivotal Game 5 in Oklahoma City with the series tied 2–2, but Chris Paul—who, again, some people consider one of the greatest point guards of all time—completely cratered in the clutch. In the final twenty seconds, he turned the ball over twice and fouled a three-point attempt by Russell Westbrook, whose three free throws gave the Thunder the lead for good. The Clippers then lost Game 6 at home.

The stain on Chris Paul's playoff legacy became permanent in 2015. The Clippers vomited all over themselves, blowing a 3–1 series lead to the Rockets, which included a nineteen-point third quarter lead in Game 6 at the Staples Center. They became just the eighth team in NBA history to blow a 3–1 lead.

In 2016 they were bounced in the first round by the Portland Trailblazers. They had a 2–0 series lead and lost four straight. The following year they were eliminated in Game 7 of the first round on their home floor to the Utah Jazz. Chris Paul shot an abysmal 6 of 19 (1 of 7 from three-point range) in that winner-take-all game. That loss marked five straight seasons in which Chris Paul and the Clippers lost a series in which they previously led. That's not an aberration. That's a trend.

Things didn't get much better when CP3 went to the Rockets. Yes, he finally made it to the Western Conference Finals in 2018, but he got hurt in Game 5 and Houston lost Games 6 and 7 without him. In 2019, they couldn't beat Golden State in the second round even after Kevin Durant left late in the third quarter of Game 5 with a calf injury. Another season ended on their home floor.

Chris Paul, this supposed all-time leader, who couldn't get along with Blake Griffin in LA, also couldn't get along with James Harden, so Houston sent Paul packing in a trade for Russell Westbrook.

CP3 finally made it to the NBA Finals in 2021 with the Phoenix Suns. The Chris Paul hive made a lot of noise, but they waved away the fact that Anthony Davis got hurt in Phoenix's first-round series against the Lakers. They ignored the fact that Jamal Murray was out for the Nuggets in the second round. And they hardly mentioned that Kawhi Leonard missed the entire Western Conference Finals for the Clippers. Three extraordinarily lucky breaks fell Phoenix's way, but those didn't get much attention, because it was a CP3 lovefest. The crowning achievement of his storied career was finally within his grasp. The validation that for years they'd said he didn't need was now on his doorstep.

Phoenix won the first two games of the Finals against the Milwaukee Bucks and the echo chamber of Chris Paul–stans grew even louder. Amin Elhassan said he had zero confidence that Milwaukee would even win a game in the series. And then the inevitable happened.

> You know what the C in Chris stands for? Choker.
> You know what the H in Chris stands for? Holding his teams back.
> You know what the R in Chris stands for? It stands for Ringless.
> You know what the I in Chris Paul stands for? It stands for I've blown more 2–0 leads than any other player in NBA history.
> You know what the S in Chris stands for? It stands for Sucks in the clutch. Which I guess is the same as choker, but shut up.

> You know what the P in Paul stands for? Payton Pritchard has more rings than I do.
> You know what the A in Paul stands for? Asphyxiates. That's different from choker because I say it is.
> You know what the U in Paul stands for? U are crazy if you think Chris Paul will ever win a title.
> You know what the L in Paul stands for? It stands for Loses whenever it matters most, which is the same as sucks in the clutch, I'll admit.

You know who has more rings than Chris Paul? Everybody who has won one.

All the great point guards who have ever played in the NBA have one thing in common: they raise championship banners. Magic Johnson: five rings; Isiah Thomas: two rings; Oscar Robertson—The Big O: one ring; Steph Curry: four rings; Jason Kidd: one ring; Tony Parker: four rings; Walt "Clyde" Frazier: two rings; Bob Cousy: six rings; Dennis Johnson—DJ: three rings; Chauncey Billups—Mr. Big Shot: one ring; Gary Payton—The Glove: one ring.

Despite the abundance of evidence to the contrary, the NBA media still fawns over Chris Paul. They call him the Point God. Point God? More like Point Fraud.

I don't even have to take away any rings from him, because he doesn't have any for me to take. But from now on he's no longer the real CP3. That moniker belongs to a true basketball great—Candace Parker, who won two titles in college and three more in the WNBA.

9

THE BIG LIE

STOP TELLING ME HOW CLOSE THE U.S. MEN'S NATIONAL TEAM is to winning the World Cup. I swear, every couple of years one of my friends who's plugged in to the soccer scene will tell me about how much better the U.S. team is now because they have this young promising striker or some upstart defender who signed with a team in the Bundesliga. They start naming players who will fill out the starting eleven and I've already stopped listening.

It's not going to happen. I'm sorry. It's just not. I've been hearing this same thing for fifty years. I'm talking back in the days when Shep Messing was in net for the New York Cosmos. This constant refrain of how the USMNT—the U.S. men's national soccer team—is just a few years away from really contending at the World Cup is a lie. I'm a Knicks fan. I know all about false hope.

Remember how Freddy Adu was supposed to be the next Pele? What about Jovan Kirovski and Jonathan Spector? They were both at Manchester United as teenagers. Oh, you've never heard of them? Me neither. U.S. soccer prodigies are a dime a dozen, but they never pan out. Wait, wasn't Julian Green supposed to be a star? What ever happened to him? Is anyone still even reading this after hearing all of those names in a row?

The United States has made it to the semifinals of the World Cup only once. That's it. Once. And that was in the inaugural World Cup back in 1930 when only thirteen countries participated. In 1930, they discovered Pluto. That's how long ago that was. And, in their semifinal match, the U.S. team was torched by Argentina 6–1. Since then the USMNT has only made it to the quarterfinals once, in 2002. This idea that they are "close" is a myth.

Chris Wittyngham, play-by-play voice of Inter Miami and former executive producer of *The Dan Le Batard Show with Stugotz*

AS WITH MOST STUGOTZ RANTS, THERE IS A KERNEL OF truth here. Yes, the expectation from some (although I'm not sure who) was that we'd wake up one morning and the world's most popular sport would be the most popular sport in the United States and we'd dominate it like we do most athletic pursuits we put our attention toward in America. 'Murica and all that.

But the answer has always been incremental gains. Stugotz says we've been at this for fifty years. Well, our first attempt at having a soccer league, the NASL, flashed brightly but eventually went out of business. Bringing over the world's biggest superstars was only worth so much without an infrastructure underneath. Many other leagues came and went before MLS—Major League Soccer—was started as a result of the 1994 World Cup. And even though MLS has had its dark moments, it's been at its best building stadia and academies that produce players better than we've ever had.

And it's working! The core of the current U.S. national teams cut their teeth here and are succeeding abroad. Weston McKennie grew up at FC Dallas and is starring for Juventus. Tyler Adams came of age at New York Red Bulls and has become a regular for Premier League–level clubs. Matt Turner changed sports in high school to proper football, was given a chance as a third-string goalkeeper at New England Revolution, and eventually worked his way to being sold to Arsenal for many millions of dollars.

Are they the best players in the world? No. It will be hard to overcome the generations of footballing tradition the major world powers lord over us. Might we never succeed at this pursuit? Maybe. It's really hard to win the World Cup. But unlike the other sports the United States dominates, we should embrace the role of underdog for once. The United States are underdogs in this sport. We will bang our heads against the wall until maybe, just maybe, proper football becomes bigger than the amateur version of the most popular sport in the country wrongly named football.

I can't believe I just entertained this argument seriously for four paragraphs.

. . .

THE REASON THE USMNT will never win the World Cup is simple. We don't care enough. We are not invested in doing what it takes to become the best soccer team in the world. It is not one of our priorities. The USMNT failed to qualify for the 2018 World Cup and only Taylor Twellman and about a handful of others were furious. The rest of us collectively yawned. We didn't care. If Brazil had failed to qualify for the World Cup the coach would have been fired immediately and there would have been a hit out on him.

Imagine if the U.S. men's basketball team failed to win gold. Well, actually, you don't have to imagine it, because it happened in 2004 in Athens. Manu Ginobili hung twenty-nine points on Stephon Marbury, Allen Iverson, and company and we went home with the bronze. That result was unacceptable to us as Americans. Team USA hired Mike Krzyzewski shortly thereafter and we have won gold at every Olympics since.

Our focus, our time, and our money are just spent elsewhere in this country. Football is the most popular sport in just about every country in the world. It is here, too, but it's an entirely different game. Soccer is, at best, the fifth most popular sport in the United States. I would argue that we like the NFL, college football, the NBA, college basketball, MLB, the NHL, golf, and maybe even tennis more than soccer.

The American public is not playing fantasy soccer. They aren't tuned in to the MLS Draft. *First Take* has never discussed the Portland Timbers. It's no surprise that our best athletes are playing other sports like football, basketball, and baseball. If soccer mattered to us like it matters to the people of Argentina or Uruguay, the next LeBron James or Russell

Westbrook would be wearing shin pads on a pitch in Anytown, USA, right now.

I just heard that there's a Soccer Hall of Fame in the United States. That building must be really empty. Now, there are plenty of U.S. women who are worthy of a hall of fame, Mia Hamm, Abby Wambach, and Alex Morgan to name a few. But who from the men's side? I can think of only two and an appendage: Tim Howard, Landon Donovan, and Christian Pulisic's penis for the goal it scored against Iran in the 2022 World Cup.

Chris Wittyngham again

THERE ARE PLENTY OF AMERICAN SOCCER LEGENDS WORthy of enshrinement for their aid in the development of the game in this country. While a nonsensical argument, it is appreciated by this reader that the anatomically correct term for Christian Pulisic's appendage was used by Stu.

DO YOU WANT TO know why Alabama is so good at football?

Because they care about football more than I care about anything except for *maybe* a new house slightly farther north. They eat, sleep, and drink Crimson Tide football. Fans wake up in the middle of February thinking about recruiting, the spring game, position battles, and what they can do to help the Tide win another national title. And it's not just the rabid fan base that is obsessed with college football supremacy. The administration, the athletic department, and the state and local governments are all aligned. Being the best college football team in the country matters to them deeply. They are all committed to winning. Alabama football is the number one driver of the economy in Tuscaloosa.

This commitment from the top down is manifested most clearly in dollars spent. Nick Saban was the highest-paid coach in the country. His assistants, in total, made more than any other staff in the country. The school spent $16 million in 2020, amid a global pandemic, to renovate the football locker room. Each locker is backlit, has a zero-gravity leather recliner, a charging station, ventilated drawers, and a lock box. That locker room is a tool for recruiting, and no team routinely spends more on recruiting than Alabama. I'm not suggesting that they paid players before the name, image, and likeness rules changed, but I'm not saying they didn't, either. The total operating budget for the football program is north of $70 million annually. No other college or university invests as much in football.

Do you know what Northwestern invests in? Their world-class graduate programs in management, education, law, and medicine. The Northwestern administration does not care about football. Sure, they'd like it if the team was good, but they don't take any ownership in the team's record. The admissions department is not letting an underqualified five-star running back into the school. The faculty is not allowing football players to turn term papers in late. Winning football games is not a priority at Northwestern like it is at Alabama. They are more focused on research grants, fostering an inclusive atmosphere on campus, and their $11 billion endowment.

Northwestern wants to produce doctors, lawyers, and Rhodes Scholars. Alabama wants to produce Heisman Trophy winners, first-round draft picks, and future Pro Bowlers. In fact,

Northwestern is better known for its alumni who cover sports than for its former athletes. Graduates of the Medill School of Journalism like my friend Mike Greenberg and my nemesis Mike Wilbon bring more awareness and prestige to Evanston than any former football players do. Hell, Northwestern's best sport is women's lacrosse, which is why my daughter went there and won a national championship.

Even without the attention, the resources, and the dedication to the football program, Pat Fitzgerald did a terrific job getting results when he was the head coach at Northwestern. In 2020, he led the Wildcats to the Big Ten title game. A win would have gotten them into the CFP, the College Football Playoff, the sport's version of the Final Four. They lost to Ohio State by double digits. It seemed like they were close, just three wins away from winning it all, but they were actually miles away.

Just like the USMNT.

The USMNT reached the quarterfinals of the World Cup in 2002. Just three wins away from winning it all. They are occasionally on the periphery of contention, like in 2002, but no one seriously thinks they have what it takes to win it all. France, Germany, Spain, Italy, and Brazil and other elite soccer countries don't view the USMNT as a real threat. They see the USMNT as a joke. To them the MLS is a league where you can collect a fat paycheck when you're well past your prime. It's like when an aging diva does a Vegas residency. Those countries are in another class.

Just like how Alabama, Clemson, Ohio State, Georgia, and USC are far superior to Northwestern. Since 1950, the Wildcats have finished in the top 10 twice. That's it. Every once in a while, they appear to be contenders. But it's an illusion.

The USMNT winning the World Cup would be the equivalent of Northwestern winning the College Football Playoff. Men's soccer is not officially dead in the United States, but that's only because it was never alive. Actually, I'm declaring it dead anyway. It's officially the first unalive thing to ever die.

10

FAKE ACE

PRETEND FOR A MINUTE THAT YOU ARE ONE OF THE MOST renowned surgeons in the world. You've written papers that have appeared in all the best medical journals. You've gotten your hospital important research grants. You've won local and national awards. Your understanding of advanced surgical technology is second to none. You make quick work of routine procedures.

All this attention has caught the eye of a certain group of celebrities. A few dozen of them schedule appointments with you. These are the highest-profile clients you've ever had. You're nervous, but you tell yourself you've been doing this same procedure for years.

Of the thirty-two celebrities you do procedures on, you completely botch thirteen of them. The surgery was in your hands, quite literally, and you made egregious mistakes. With that on your résumé, would anyone still consider you the greatest surgeon in the world?

Of course not. And that's Clayton Kershaw.

Kershaw is an outstanding pitcher in the regular season. He's racked up three Cy Young Awards, and in 2014 became the first NL pitcher to be named MVP since Bob Gibson in 1968. His career earned run average is 2.48, which is lower than those of Greg Maddux (3.16), Roger Clemens (3.12), Pedro Martinez (2.93), Randy Johnson (3.29), Sandy Koufax (2.76), and the aforementioned Gibson (2.91). He stacks up ahead of some of the all-time greats.

The problem with suggesting that Kershaw is one of the greatest pitchers of all time, though, is that when the pressure of the playoffs arrives and the stakes get raised, he crumbles.

Kershaw's postseason ERA, as of this writing, is 4.49. That's more than two full runs higher than his regular-season ERA. This isn't the case of some small sample size, either. Kershaw has pitched nearly two hundred innings in the playoffs. He has repeatedly faltered on the biggest stage. When it comes time to sink or swim, he plummets. True greats swim. And they swim fast.

MICHAEL PHELPS QUALIFIED FOR the Olympics when he was fifteen. He didn't win any medals, but he finished fifth in the 200-meter butterfly. He was a phenom. Phelps continued his upward trajectory at the World Championships in 2001 and

2003, winning races and setting new records along the way, but the public doesn't care about the World Championships. The public only pays attention to the Olympics. That is the showcase event.

Phelps entered the 2004 Olympic games in Athens with all kinds of hype. Even with the weight of the lofty expectations and the added media scrutiny, he delivered. Phelps took home six gold medals and two bronze. He cemented his place as one of the greatest U.S. Olympians ever, but no one was calling him the greatest. Not yet, anyway. The greatest was Mark Spitz, who won seven golds in Munich in 1972.

Every day for four years Michael Phelps had to hear about falling just short of Spitz's record. That made the burden of expectations even higher for Phelps at the 2008 Olympics in Beijing. He couldn't make any mistakes. Not one. And with the pressure of the moment amplified and the stakes raised as high as they could possibly go, he was flawless. Eight gold medals. Eight new Olympic record times. Phelps bested Spitz and became the greatest U.S. Olympic athlete of all time.

Kershaw is Michael Phelps if he never won a gold medal at the Olympics.

Yet, somehow some people treat him like he's the best to ever do it. Not only is Kershaw's postseason ERA (4.49) nearly a run higher than those of some of the all-time greats—Maddux (3.27), Clemens (3.75), Pedro (3.46), Randy Johnson (3.50), Koufax (0.95), and Gibson (1.89)—he's also the only one of the group who hasn't won the World Series.

Kershaw even pales in comparison to some of his contemporaries. Madison Bumgarner, another left-handed career National Leaguer, has won three World Series (and been named the MVP of one of them) and has a career postseason ERA of 2.11. Max Scherzer, who has won as many Cy Young Awards as Kershaw (three), led the Nationals to the 2019 World Series and has a career postseason ERA of 3.38.

The 2019 postseason was particularly damning for Kershaw. He started and lost Game 2 of the National League Division Series to the Nationals. Then in the decisive Game 5, Los Angeles manager Dave Roberts turned to Kershaw to protect a 3–1 lead. He struck out the first batter he faced to get out of the seventh. Then he blew the lead by allowing back-to-back home runs to start the eighth. The Nats won the game in the tenth inning to advance to the NLCS. Kershaw allowed as many home runs in the eighth inning as Mariano Rivera (legitimately one of the greatest pitchers of all time) allowed in his entire postseason career, having faced 527 batters.

In 2023, Kershaw gave up six earned runs on six hits and recorded just one out in a Game 1 start against the Diamondbacks in the Division Series. That was good for an ERA of 162.00.

There is no disputing Clayton Kershaw's greatness in the regular season. I see it. There is plenty of disputing his overall greatness, which weights the postseason heavily. In his career after the sixth inning, Kershaw has an ERA of 2.33 in the regular season and an ERA of 12.27 in the postseason, which is the highest of all time (counting those with a minimum of ten innings pitched).

Kershaw cannot be considered a top 20 pitcher of all time. Pitchers are supposed to be preventing runs in the postseason, not getting them in their pants.

Greatness is earned when it matters most. Not on a Tuesday in May against the Padres.

Tim Kurkjian, ESPN MLB Insider who was honored with the BBWAA Career Excellence Award by the Hall of Fame in 2022

TO BORROW A LINE FROM JIM PALMER, WHO ONCE SAID OF Earl Weaver, his brilliant Hall of Fame manager, "The only thing that Earl knows about pitching is that he couldn't hit it." And then there is Stugotz, who knows absolutely nothing about pitching . . . or hitting . . . or the history of baseball . . . or how hard the game is to play.

Clayton Kershaw is one of the twenty best pitchers in major league history. A dear friend who does stats for a living has him as the sixth-best pitcher since 1913, the year that ERA became an official statistic. My friend has him above Warren Spahn, Tom Seaver, Randy Johnson, Pedro Martinez, and, eleventh on the list, Jim Palmer, who, even I acknowledge, is no longer the best baseball player ever to wear No. 22. Kershaw is.

ERA is, for me, the best barometer of a pitcher's effectiveness. Kershaw's 2.48 ERA is the lowest of any starting pitcher in the Live Ball Era, from 1920 on. Kershaw's career record is 210–92, a winning percentage of .695—no other pitcher in major league history has ever had a winning percentage that high with an ERA that low.

Of course, there is more: three Cy Young Awards, two seconds, a third, and a fifth. A career WHIP of 1.004 and 9.8 strikeouts per nine innings in his career. In 2015, then-Giants pitcher Madison Bumgarner wondered aloud, "Are we watching the greatest pitcher of all time?" No, we are not—that honor belongs to Walter Johnson. What we are watching is a top 10 pitcher from 1913 on, and, no doubt, a top 20 ever.

Interestingly, Bumgarner is one of the greatest postseason pitchers of all time. And, Stugotz, for once, is right: Kershaw is not. There is no denying some of his failures in the postseason: a 13–13 record and a 4.49 ERA. But, this is baseball. The game is so hard to play, it is filled with players who weren't as great in the postseason as in the regular season. Randy Johnson, a top 10 pitcher of all time, went 0–7 during an eight-start stretch early in his postseason career. Roger Clemens, maybe the second-best pitcher ever, had a 3.75 ERA in the postseason. Greg Maddux, a top 5 pitcher ever, had an 11–14 record in the postseason. Clemens, Maddux, Johnson, and Pedro Martinez are a combined 36–35 in their postseason careers. This is not basketball, which I love. No great NBA player averages twenty-five a game in the regular season, but in the playoffs averages eight points. Only in baseball are the best players occasionally beaten by the game in October.

And in 2020, when the Dodgers won the World Series, Kershaw was terrific. That season cemented his legacy as the greatest Dodger pitcher ever, even better than Sandy Koufax. Kershaw has more strikeouts than any other pitcher in the rich history of the Dodgers, and his name says so: an anagram for Clayton Kershaw is LA K Hero Wants Cy. An anagram for Stugotz is: Stu Got Z. The Z is for zero.

The Rebuttal to the Rebuttal

Hey, Tim, thank you so much. Quick question. This friend you mentioned? Is his name Clayton Kershaw?

11

NADA(L)

SOME PEOPLE WOULD HAVE YOU BELIEVE THAT WE JUST LIVED through the golden age of men's tennis. The Big Three of Roger Federer, Rafael Nadal, and Novak Djokovic each won twenty or more Grand Slams between 2003 and 2023. Before that, no one in the history of men's tennis had ever won more than fourteen. Surely, they are the three best players of all time, right?

Well, when you start to dig just a little bit deeper into the history of the Big Three, something jumps out and leaves you questioning everything that you've been led to believe. It's startling, really. Are you sitting down? OK, good. Now take a deep breath. Ready? Read this next sentence slowly. Rafael Nadal won the French Open fourteen times. Fourteen! I just got done telling you that no one outside of the Big Three had ever won more than fourteen total Grand Slams and he's won the French Open on fourteen different occasions? Pretty fishy.

The French Open is a weird tournament. It is. It's played on clay, which is odd. Clay is used to make bricks, pottery, and former Miami Dolphin tight ends. But they play tennis on it? The tournament is held at a place called Roland Garros, which until this very moment I did not know was the name of a French aviator. That's strange. The US Open is played at Arthur Ashe Stadium and Ashe was a famous U.S. tennis player. The Australian Open is played in Rod Laver Arena and Laver was a famous Aussie tennis player. The French Open is played at Roland Garros and Garros was a pilot in World War I with no connection to tennis? Weird tournament.

So they play it on a weird surface in France at a place named after an aviator instead of a tennis player, and these are the guys who've won multiple times. Ready? Max Decugis. You ever heard of him? He's won it eight times. OK, Henri Cochet. You ever heard of him? Five-time winner. André Vacherot? Heard of him? Four times. Mats Wilander. Three times. Gustavo Kuerten. Three times. Sergi Bruguera. Wins it two times. It's a weird tournament where weird guys will win it multiple times, because it's a totally different brand of tennis. In fact, it's not even tennis. It's so weird that a Frenchman hasn't won it since Yannick Noah in 1983. And he produced Joakim Noah. Like I said, weird tournament.

Honestly, it's too weird of a tournament to be considered a major. I'm sorry. It just is. This would be like if The Masters were held at a par-3 course. You're simply not getting the best of the best at a gimmicky venue like Roland Garros with red clay on the ground. You're getting Sergi Bruguera and Mats Wilander multiple times. You know that's wrong. You *know* it. There's something up with it.

The French Open is no longer a Grand Slam. I know the French are quick to wave the white flag, but it's not like I'm asking them to completely surrender their tournament. They can still host it. It just isn't a major anymore.

From now on, here's how I treat the all-time greats. Take all their Slams, subtract any French Open titles, and stack them up from there.

And what do you know? You get a much better representation of tennis excellence.

Novak Djokovic—21
Roger Federer—19
Pete Sampras—14
Roy Emerson—10
Big Bill Tilden—10
Rod Laver—9
Rafael Nadal—8

So, when it comes to the Mount Rushmore of men's tennis, the Joker, Federer, and Sampras are locks, but I've got news for Roy Emerson and Big Bill Tilden: Rod Laver is getting that fourth spot, and here's why. There's a reason the Australian Open named its arena after Laver and not his contemporary countryman, Emerson. Laver won five majors and then turned pro in 1963. For whatever reason, professionals weren't allowed to compete in majors until 1968, when the Open Era began. So Laver missed out on twenty-one chances to win more majors, in his prime, because he turned pro.

And guess when Emerson won eight of his ten Slams? Yup, in the five years Laver wasn't eligible to compete. So, I think, conservatively speaking, Laver would have won at least four more, which puts him at thirteen and gets his face carved into a mountain of all-time male tennis greats.

Now back to Nadal. He's still one of the best tennis players of all time. Eight Grand Slam titles is nothing to sneeze at. Rafa just falls more into the Charles Barkley category now—a great player who was overshadowed throughout his career by someone, or in Nadal's case, two guys, even greater.

If Nadal were smart, he would have spread out some of his Slams. He would have sprinkled a couple more US Opens in, a couple of Wimbledons in, a few less French Opens, and then he'd be on the Mount Rushmore of men's tennis. Instead he's on the Mount Rushmore of winning a weird tournament. Along with Henri Cochet.

Mardy Fish, who won a silver medal in men's tennis at the 2004 Olympics, won six times on the ATP Tour, and made it to the quarterfinals in every slam except the French Open. Fish went 1–8 in his career against Rafael Nadal.

WOW, THAT'S A TOUGH READ. I DON'T EVEN KNOW WHERE to begin, so I'll start with the idea that the French Open isn't a Grand Slam in this ridiculous record book.

The French Open is the toughest Grand Slam to win in tennis. The amount of physical fitness, mental toughness, and, oh, the fact that you have to be better than everyone else

at actual tennis puts this ahead of the US Open in terms of toughest to win. Five grueling sets against guys who grew up on that surface is brutally hard. You have to do this for seven straight matches over the course of fourteen days. And don't even think about playing a Frenchman or woman in the event. The crowd will scream and whistle at you and tell you how much you suck for five straight hours. Weather can be anywhere from cold and windy to extremely hot and humid in late May/early June.

Clay is a very specialized surface. It's a surface that requires an incredible amount of physical fitness. Hours upon hours on the court daily, followed by hours of fitness and rehab on your body. This is every day. Miss a day, you are behind everyone else. Clay is also a surface where you cannot rely on free points. Meaning, having a big serve or big groundstrokes to rely on doesn't work nearly as well on this surface. The crushed brick you talked about makes the ball bounce more slowly and also, at times, funkily and awkwardly. Movement on the surface is also extremely difficult, with slipping and sliding around all over the place.

These facts alone make it one of the toughest trophies to win in all of sports. It's certainly the toughest tennis trophy to win, in my eyes. And if you wave it away as a Grand Slam with whatever fake magic wand you gave yourself, then you would be doing the very thing you hate the most from athletes: taking the easy path.

So that brings us to Rafa—by *far* the greatest clay court player of all time: 112-3 all time. That's not a misprint: 112 and THREE! Of his fourteen titles at Roland Garros, he did not drop a set in the entire tournament FOUR times! And three other times he only lost one set. Meaning that in seven of his fourteen titles, he lost only three total sets. It's truly hard to comprehend. My guess is that if Rafa weren't around, Roger and Novak would have seven or eight French Open titles each.

Stugotz, the only Grand Slam you should talk about with any authority is the one from Denny's. Certainly not the hallowed grounds of Roland Garros.

Maybe stick to lacrosse or something, buddy.

The Rebuttal to the Rebuttal

TOP 5 ATHLETES AND ENTERTAINERS WHO CONNOTE A FISH

OLI

Mardy Fish

5. Greg Norman (The Shark)
4. Brandon Bass
3. Tim Salmon
2. Catfish Hunter
1. Mike Trout

12

THE GREEK FEAT

SOMETHING INCREDIBLY RARE HAPPENED IN THE SUMMER OF 2021. So rare, some might call it freakish.

In an era in which NBA players routinely demand trades, force their way out of situations, and team up with their All-Star friends to form super teams, one guy stayed put and Milwaukee Bucked the trend.

Giannis Antetokounmpo—The Greek Freak—put the Milwaukee Bucks on his back and won the Larry O'Brien Trophy. There is simply no denying that he did it all by himself. That Bucks team was handing out significant minutes to Pat Connaughton, Bryn Forbes, the ghost of Jeff Teague, and Bobby Portis, who to that point did more damage to his teammates' faces than to opponents. There were no other stars on the team.

Sure, Jrue Holiday had made the All-Star Game eight seasons prior. So did Brook Lopez. And Khris Middleton made two All-Star Games, but only because the Bucks needed to be rewarded for having a great record that Giannis led them to. Go ahead and build a team around Khris Middleton. I dare you. That team would not even sniff the play-in tournament.

As if Giannis's back wasn't carrying enough of the load, he also had to throw his coach on there. After blowing a 2–0 lead in the 2019 Conference Finals to the Raptors and then losing to the fifth-seeded Heat in the second round in the bubble, Bucks coach Mike Budenholzer, who looks like a sad-faced clown who has trouble removing all his makeup, was on the hot seat. Sources told me at the time that if the Bucks didn't at least make the Finals, Coach Bud was going to be the fall guy and get axed. So not only did Giannis lead the Bucks to a title, he also saved his coach's job.

Quite frankly, Giannis did what any truly great player should do. He took the hard path. He was drafted by the Bucks in 2015 and he eventually brought them a championship. He never pouted. He never demanded a trade. Even after winning back-to-back MVPs, he wasn't critical of the front office for failing to surround him with better players. He put his nose to the grindstone, got better, made The Climb, and ultimately reached the mountaintop.

What made the Bucks' title run so rare was that it was just the second time since 1980 in which a team won the NBA championship with less than two future Hall of Famers on its roster. Again, Giannis was out there with Bobby Portis and the ghost of Jeff Teague.

In 2019, Kawhi Leonard led the Raptors to the title, but they only won it all because the Warriors were without Kevin Durant (he came back in Game 6 for twelve minutes and tore his Achilles) and Klay Thompson, who tore his ACL in Game 6.

That's the entire list.

And let's not forget the fashion in which Giannis dragged Pat Connaughton, Bryn Forbes, and company across the finish line.

Giannis left Game 4 of the Conference Finals with a hyperextended knee injury. There were serious questions about whether he was done for the remainder of the playoffs.

Like the freak that he is, Giannis returned seven days later for the Finals against the Phoenix Suns. The Bucks lost the first two games on the road, at which point Amin Elhassan said he had zero confidence that Milwaukee would even win a game in the series. The better take would have been to say that the Suns wouldn't win another game in the series, because they had that fraud Chris Paul running the show.

The Bucks held serve at home thanks to an all-time Giannis block of Deandre Ayton at the rim to seal Game 4. Then they won Game 5 in Phoenix courtesy of an alley-oop to Giannis in the final seconds to secure the win.

With a chance to win the title at home in Game 6, Giannis put on one of the greatest finals performances in NBA history. He scored fifty points on twenty-five shots, grabbed fourteen rebounds, blocked five shots, and dished out a couple of assists. Perhaps more remarkably, he went 17 of 19 from the free throw line (89 percent). Prior to Game 6, he was shooting a frigid 55 percent from the line. But with the Larry O'Brien Trophy in the building, Giannis bucked up and single-handedly grabbed it.

Do you know what the G in Giannis stands for? Gutted it out.

Do you know what the A in Antetokounmpo stands for? The Anti-Durant.

The fifty-burger in the closeout game wasn't even Giannis's most impressive feat that summer. With COVID-19 still rampaging throughout the United States, most of the city of Milwaukee decided to gather outside of the Bucks' arena, in what they called the Deer District, to watch the games. I have it on good authority that the Deer District is where the Omicron variant was spawned. All those Wisconsinites rubbing elbows and high-fiving with their cheese-baked hands. How Giannis managed to stay dry in the eye of that storm I'll never know.

For winning a title by himself in the super-team era and avoiding COVID-19 during the playoffs while playing next to the Deer District, Giannis gets two rings.

With two rings and two MVPs, Giannis is officially a member of my All-European team.

ALL-EUROPEAN TEAM

PG—Tony Parker
SG—Drazen Petrovic
SF—Toni Kukoc
PF—Dirk Nowitzki
C—Giannis Antetokounmpo
Sixth Man—Pau Gasol
Seventh Man—Peja Stojakovic

13

KEEP AWAY

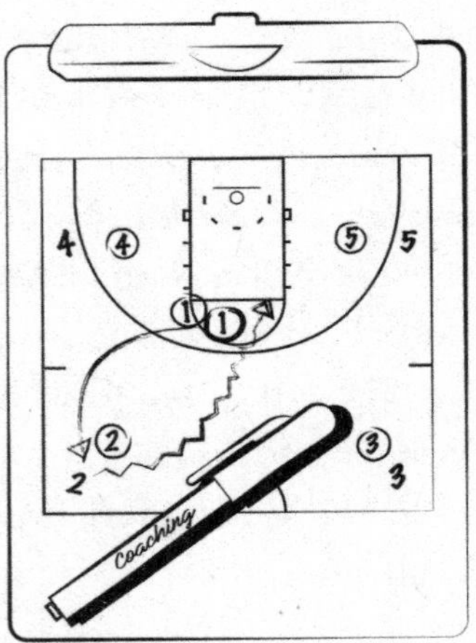

WHAT IF I TOLD YOU THAT THE GLASS SLIPPER DIDN'T FIT? That Cinderella left the dance and turned into a pumpkin. That Goliath slayed David. That the hare destroyed the tortoise.

April 1, 1985. Rupp Arena. Lexington, Kentucky.

A Big East battle between the eighth-seeded Villanova Wildcats and the first-seeded Georgetown Hoyas.

Most people operate under the assumption that Villanova won the NCAA Men's Basketball National Championship that night, but I've got news for you. They didn't. I mean, they won something that night, but it wasn't a basketball game. If it was the NCAA Tournament for playing keep-away, then Villanova was the most deserving champion.

Unfortunately, it was the NCAA Men's Basketball Tournament. And they didn't play basketball. They played anything but basketball. They were trying not to play basketball. It's absurd the lengths they went to avoid playing basketball. Their attempt to win a game of basketball by not playing basketball was unforgivable. They went too far.

There's no argument you could make that the better team that year wasn't the team that had Patrick Ewing. That had David Wingate. That had Reggie Williams. That had Michael Jackson. The point guard. Not the pop singer. That was the better basketball team, OK? Unfortunately, the better basketball team didn't get to play much basketball in the second half. What they spent most of their time doing was trying to get the ball away from a bunch of guys who were playing some kind of professional version of hot potato. That ain't basketball. Get the hell out of here.

Villanova lucked their way into a one-point lead at the half. They shot an unfathomable 72 percent from the floor that included a shot by Harold Pressley that bounced off the rim more times than Kawhi Leonard's game-winner in 2019 against the Sixers. With a one-point advantage, the Wildcats decided to stop playing basketball altogether for the final twenty minutes. Villanova took only ten shots in the entire second half. Ten! Ten shots in twenty minutes is nothing. Dion Waiters could get ten shots up in three possessions. In the 2022 NCAA Men's National Championship game, North Carolina led Kansas by fifteen at halftime. The Tar Heels still attempted forty shots in the second half. That's four times as many as Villanova attempted.

If the Seven Seconds or Less Phoenix Suns advanced the sport of basketball into the future, then the 1985 Villanova Wildcats set the sport back multiple decades. Thankfully, basketball was not affected, though, because Villanova was not playing basketball.

My apologies, and with all due respect, and may God rest his soul, but, Rollie Massimino, you did not win a national championship. And you should be ashamed of yourself. Again, all due respect. Harold Pressley, you did not win a national championship. Dwayne McClain, you didn't either. The other McClain, you didn't win one either. And, Ed Pinckney, you were actually good at basketball. Unfortunately, you were on a team that wasn't playing basketball. You didn't win a national championship either.

I take no pride in stripping away a championship from the Wildcats. It's a Villa-no-fun thing to do, but it's what must be done. You can't be the champions in basketball if you refused to play it.

There's a reason the NCAA implemented a shot clock the very next season. Villanova's keep-away act was so obvious that even an organization with as many blind spots as the NCAA was able to identify the absurdity.

Go watch the second half of the game online and tell me what you see. I'll wait here. You back? Did you see people playing basketball? You did not. And if you say you did, I can't hear you anyway. But you can hear me say this: you're wrong.

And so I present to you the 1985 Men's Basketball National Champions: the Georgetown Hoyas. How about that? I mean, a little extra ring for John Thompson, Jr. An extra ring for Patrick Ewing. You are welcome. And, Patrick—I know you didn't win a title with the Knicks, but that's not on you. That's on Charles Smith for missing four bunnies against the Bulls in '93.

Jay Bilas, ESPN college basketball analyst, who played in the 1985 Men's Basketball Tournament for a Duke team that was a #3 seed and lost in the second round

NO OFFENSE, STUGOTZ, BUT THIS IS STUPID.

The 1985 NCAA championship game between Villanova and Georgetown was not just a memorable upset; it qualifies as one of the greatest upsets in Final Four history, if not THE greatest. While NC State beating Houston in 1983 ranks right up there, Villanova's win over mighty Georgetown was as close to pitching a perfect game against the 1927 Yankees as one could get in basketball.

We all know that you have thrown away brain cells as cavalierly as you throw away strokes on the golf course, the only place you are able to destroy private property while intoxicated without being arrested. For this "hot take," you should be arrested and charged with drunk and disorderly, and the use of excessive force is justified. One would have to be fall-down drunk to even consider denigrating Rollie Massimino's masterpiece, let alone doing so in writing.

In 1985, there was indeed no shot clock, yet Villanova and Georgetown combined for 130 points in Villanova's 66–64 win. That total was more than North Carolina and Georgetown scored in 1982 when Dean Smith won his first title, more than Indiana and North Carolina scored when Bob Knight won his second title, and more than Louisville and UCLA scored when Denny Crum won his first title. And, it was more than NC State and Houston scored in Jim

Valvano's historic title run in 1983. Should those miserable pikers give back their wins under the same asinine theory? Of course not. If your standard were applied to all, and your standards are usually quite low, John Wooden, Jim Calhoun, Mike Krzyzewski, and Gary Williams would all have to forfeit titles (and the last three fell short of Villanova's totals WITH a shot clock).

Villanova shot 22 of 28 from the field against one of the best and most intimidating defenses in the college game. Georgetown boasted five future NBA players and an all-time great in Patrick Ewing. The Wildcats' near-perfect game was less about the shot clock and more about execution. Speaking of execution, yours should be quickly scheduled based upon this idiotic missive.

Should your mindless, imbecilic, half-witted . . . no, quarter-witted submission gain any steam among your demented following, you will next need to start your campaign to invalidate the titles of Wooden, Smith, Knight, Krzyzewski, Crum, Calhoun, and others. After all, a standard is a standard. And, a moron is a moron.

I have reconsidered my opening line. Take offense, Stugotz, this is stupid.

The Rebuttal to the Rebuttal

Offense? That's something we didn't see from Villanova in the second half of the 1985 National Championship Game.

14

MR. LIMITED

THE SEATTLE SEAHAWKS HIT A HOME RUN WHEN THEY DRAFTED Russell Wilson in the third round of the 2012 NFL Draft. As a rookie he beat out prized free agent Matt Flynn for the job. I know that sounds crazy, but Flynn was the backup in Green Bay and looked great in a meaningless Week 17 game against the Lions, so every quarterback-needy team wanted him. Seattle gave him a bunch of money, but then realized that the 5-foot-11 kid they drafted out of Wisconsin was better. Kudos to head coach Pete Carroll for admitting the organization's mistake and giving the keys to Wilson right out of the gate, because that decision led to the greatest era in franchise history.

What Wilson lacked in size he made up for in leadership, escapability, and a deft touch with the deep ball. In ten years in Seattle, Wilson led the Seahawks to nine playoff wins, including

Super Bowl XLVIII. I know I just praised Pete Carroll, but now I have to rip him because he and offensive coordinator Darrell Bevell choked on the greatest stage and cost the Seahawks another Super Bowl. Instead of just handing the ball to Marshawn Lynch on the 1-yard line with twenty-five ticks left, they outthought the room and decided to throw it. Wilson's pass was intercepted by Malcolm Butler and the Patriots and Tom Brady won Super Bowl XLIX. I hate them.

Even with the worst-timed turnover in Super Bowl history, Wilson was everything you would have wanted in a franchise quarterback. He made nine Pro Bowls, led the league in passing in 2017, finished top four in Offensive Player of the Year voting three separate times, and was named as the Walter Payton NFL Man of the Year in 2020. He never got in trouble off the field. In fact, the headlines he drew were mostly about four things: 1) His marriage to Grammy winner Ciara; 2) How it was possible that he never received an MVP vote; 3) His corny habit of practicing huddles, high fives, and two-minute drills against air; and 4) Why the Seahawks should let him cook.

Russell Wilson was on a collision course with Canton. It was a lock. Five years after he retired, Wilson was going to get the bust, don the gold jacket, ride in the parade, and deliver the most boring induction speech in the history of the Pro Football Hall of Fame. He was a proven winner at the hardest position in sports. In his first nine years in Seattle, he led the Seahawks to double-digit regular-season wins and a playoff berth eight times. The one time they failed to make the postseason they still went 9–7.

But instead of getting the bust, it all went bust. In March 2022, Wilson waived his no-trade clause and was dealt to the

Denver Broncos for Drew Lock, Noah Fant, Shelby Harris, two first-round picks, two second-round picks, and a fifth-round pick. Seattle sold high on their franchise quarterback and did so at the perfect time.

Russ did not cook in his first year in Denver. He looked cooked. In Week 1, Wilson went back to his old stomping grounds in Seattle and got stomped by Geno Smith and the Seahawks, who would go on to make the playoffs. Things didn't get much better from there. The Broncos started 3–12 and Wilson was an abject disaster. He threw a career-low sixteen TD passes, posted a career-low QBR of 36.7, and was sacked a league high fifty-five times despite playing in only fifteen games.

It's not like he didn't have weapons, either. Jerry Jeudy was a first-round pick, Courtland Sutton was a Pro Bowler, and Melvin Gordon was coming off a season where he rushed for over 900 yards while splitting time with Javonte Williams.

It probably didn't help that he was the consolation prize for the Broncos. Denver had their hopes set on landing Aaron Rodgers. They even went as far as to hire his offensive coordinator, Nathaniel Hackett, to be their new head coach. Rodgers stayed in Green Bay for one more season and the Broncos moved on to plan B: Russell Wilson.

Hackett couldn't hack it and was fired after the season, but he hardly had a chance with the way Wilson played. Russ went 4–11 in his first season as the Broncos' starting quarterback. To put things in perspective, Tim Tebow went 8–6 with the Broncos. Hell, Brock Osweiler went 5–2. *Brock. Osweiler.*

It's unfair to eggs to say that Wilson laid one in 2022. His season was such a stinker that his Hall of Fame case completely crumbled. Before 2022 he was in. No questions asked. In 2022, he was so bad that he played his way out. No questions asked. He shat the bed so badly that it reeked up the rest of his résumé. The drop-off from his performance in Seattle to his performance in year one in Denver was disturbing. Appalling. The kind of drop-off that makes you question life itself. The only other cliff dive that dramatic is Francis Ford Coppola before and after *Apocalypse Now*. All-incredible to all-dogshit in an instant.

Go look at the all-time great quarterbacks. None have seasons as pitiful as Wilson's 2022 campaign.

The best test as to whether someone is or isn't a Hall of Famer is your immediate reaction when you hear a question like, Russell Wilson: Hall of Famer? Before the 2022 season it was such an easy and obvious yes. Now, the mention of his name brings an instant air of disgust.

Wilson is a religious man (so much so that he'd probably be pissed that I put him in the same sentence as the term Plan B), so I'll grant him absolution. I'm willing to wipe the slate clean. His horrendous first season with the Broncos is gone. But so is everything he accomplished in the NFL through the 2022 season. Poof. No Super Bowl, no Pro Bowls, no nothing. If he wants to get into the Hall of Fame, it will be based on what he does from 2023 on.

And 2023 was no picnic. Even Super Bowl–winning head coach Sean Payton, a known quarterback guru who took over as Broncos head coach in 2023, couldn't resurrect Wilson's career. Wilson was benched late in the season and then outright released in the offseason.

Mina Kimes: ESPN NFL analyst, host of *The Mina Kimes Show featuring Lenny*, and a diehard Seahawks fan

I HAVE NO IDEA HOW STUGOTZ CONVINCED ME TO TAKE on the assignment of defending Russell Wilson, the quarterback who left the team I've rooted for my entire life. Enlisting a Seahawks fan to go to bat for Russ these days is a little like asking an ex to give you an endorsement on your Tinder profile. Eventually, I'll get over the breakup . . . but things are still a little weird between us! And yet, while my fandom for the player is complicated, I will never stop rooting for FACTS and NUMBERS, so I'll attempt to rebut the argument of a friend who has a tenuous relationship with both of those concepts.

Let's start with Russ's case for the Hall. It isn't open-and-shut. He's never been league MVP or even a first-team All-Pro. But he is a Super Bowl champion and nine-time Pro Bowler, and he ranks in the top twenty of all time in passing yards, touchdowns, and passer rating. While some of that production does stem from the quarterback-friendly era he plays in, Russ also ranks twentieth in wins (I realize that I've spent most of my career arguing that wins aren't a quarterback stat . . . but they matter to the Hall! The Stugotz is strong in me, I guess).

Regardless of how well Wilson plays in the future, most of those numbers will continue to rise, and it'll be hard to exclude a Super Bowl champion who ranks in the top ten or fifteen of most significant passing categories, especially since so many quarterbacks who are already in the Hall rank way below him.

Also . . . about those quarterbacks. Stu wrote that there's never been a player in the Hall whose performance took a dive like Wilson's did during his first season in Denver. That's not true! There are a number of enshrined players whose numbers dropped like a twelve-year-old boy's vocal cords toward the end of their careers. I'll name one: Fran Tarkenton, the Vikings quarterback who's occasionally compared to Russ because of their diminutive size. In his final year with the Vikings, Tarkenton—who has zero Super Bowl rings, by the way—threw a whopping THIRTY-TWO interceptions, which led the league that year and ranks fourth all time. To put that in perspective, Jameis Winston was ridiculed for throwing thirty picks (the infamous thirty-for-thirty year).

And yet: Tarkenton is in the Hall.

I mentioned some of the numbers that support Russ's case, but his qualifications aren't wholly quantifiable. As a 5-foot-10 quarterback drafted in the third round who used his legs as much as anyone early in his career, he helped change the paradigm for the position. While there were a few exceptions (notably Michael Vick) to the prototypical pocket passer stereotype before Russ, it seemed impossible that anyone under six feet could play quarterback at a high level in the NFL. Since then, we've seen less of an emphasis on height and a greater embrace of mobility across the league.

Stu's anti-Russ argument reeks of recency bias, which makes sense coming from someone who probably forgets what he had for breakfast by dinnertime (cigarettes, I'd guess). But he's wrong. Regardless of what happened in

2022 and what happens in 2024 and beyond, Wilson's already done enough to merit strong consideration for the Hall. And that should mean a lot coming from me, given what's transpired in recent years . . . but I didn't ask for any of this!

15

LEFTY

I LOVE GOLF. IT'S MY FAVORITE SPORT TO PLAY AND IT'S MY favorite sport to watch. Hitting a golf shot exactly how you intended to, or watching one hit purely, is something like a religious experience. And the High Holy Days in my house involve Amen Corner. I am completely enraptured every April when the best in the world gather at Augusta National for The Masters. It's the most prestigious of the four majors. No disrespect to the PGA Championship, the US Open, and the Open Championship, but there's just something about Augusta National that feels majestic. I'm sure that being the only major that's played at the same course every year adds to the allure, but the picturesque views, Verne Lundquist in the tower at the sixteenth hole, the history, the tradition, and Jim Nantz welcoming all his friends to the broadcast like a priest at church make it the cathedral of golf.

The hairs on my forearms rise just by writing about The Masters.

While we have consensus about The Masters being the best of the four majors, we don't have consensus about the greatest men to ever tee it up. The top three, to me, are easy.

1. Jack Nicklaus—The Golden Bear. Jack's eighteen majors are three more than anyone else. He's one of five golfers to complete the career Grand Slam (winning all four majors) and one of only two golfers to achieve a triple Grand Slam (winning all four majors at least three times). His seventy-three wins on the PGA Tour rank third all time.
2. Tiger Woods. Tiger has a case if you're talking about the most influential golfers of all time, but he's a clear second to Jack. And I love Tiger. I wear a red shirt every Sunday, but I don't close nearly as often as Tiger did. Tiger is second in majors with fifteen and tied for first with eighty-two wins on the PGA Tour. He is the only other golfer to achieve the triple Grand Slam.
3. Arnold Palmer. Arnie is tied for seventh when it comes to major championships with seven, but he's fifth in wins on the PGA Tour (sixty-two), and a runaway winner in likability. He was a true ambassador of the game and became the most beloved golfer because of it. His rise came about in conjunction with the majority of Americans getting televisions. Arnie's

Army, his massive fan base, is rivaled only by the legion of Tiger Woods fans. Plus, he made up that delicious drink. Half lemonade. Half iced tea. Genius.

The fourth spot among the best in golf is unclear to most, but not to me. Some don't even put Arnie third, which is sacrilegious. Other names often considered for the last spot on the Mount Rushmore include Walter Hagen (third all time with eleven major championships), Ben Hogan (fourth in both majors with nine and wins with sixty-five), Sam Snead (tied for first with eighty-two wins and seventh in majors with seven), Gary Player (tied for fourth in majors with nine and a major influence on the growth of the sport internationally), Tom Watson (sixth in majors with eight), and Bobby Jones (tied for seventh in majors with seven despite never playing in the PGA, and also co-founded The Masters). Those guys were all great, but none of them are the fourth-best golfer of all time.

The fourth-best golfer of all time is Phil Mickelson. Lefty. He's won six majors, which puts him in a tie for twelfth all time, and he's won forty-five times on the PGA Tour, which is good for eighth. I know what you're thinking. If he's twelfth in majors and eighth in wins, then how the hell is he the fourth-best golfer of all time?

For starters, Phil won his six majors in the Tiger Woods era. Tiger may not be the greatest golfer of all time, but he was certainly the most dominant. Tiger vs. the field was a legitimate (and profitable) bet. That's how much he dominated the game. The fact that Phil was able to win six majors is incredible. They carry more weight because of the era in which he won them.

Tiger was also a robot both on and off the course. No one could relate to him. People could relate to Phil, though. While

Tiger was doing Navy SEALS training, Phil's weight was fluctuating, much like that of most Americans. Phil had (has?) a gambling problem, just like a lot of Americans, probably (definitely?) even you at home reading this. Tiger was worshipped. His greatness put him on a pedestal. He was almost godlike. He was not accessible. Phil was likable. He was one of us. Tiger was Goliath. Phil was David.

Aside from being the closest thing to a rival of the most dominant player in the sport, Phil's career has been full of near misses. Mickelson has finished second in major championships twelve times, including six times at the US Open, which is the only major he has failed to win. The only person with more runner-up finishes in majors is Jack Nicklaus, with nineteen. Being that close to more majors is not a knock. Phil did not choke things away twelve times. All right, he choked at the US Open in 2006 at Winged Foot. You can't have a one-shot lead on the seventy-second hole, make a double bogey, and lose to Geoff Ogilvy. The other eleven second-place finishes, though, were not choke jobs. He got himself in position to win and things didn't fall his way.

If you add up every golfer's major victories and their second-place finishes in majors, you'd have a better idea of who was consistently great over time. That list looks like this:

Jack Nicklaus: 18 majors, 19 runner-ups—37
Tiger Woods: 15 majors, 7 runner-ups—22
Phil Mickelson: 6 majors, 12 runner-ups—18
Arnold Palmer: 7 majors, 10 runner-ups—17
Tom Watson: 8 majors, 8 runner-ups—16
Gary Player: 9 majors, 6 runner-ups—15
Ben Hogan: 9 majors, 6 runner-ups—15

Tiger's dominance unquestionably ushered in a new era of golf where strength, power, and youth ruled the day. Dustin Johnson, Brooks Koepka, Rory McIlroy, and Jon Rahm have all won multiple majors hitting the ball a mile. The crop of young, talented players in the game has never been stronger. And yet Phil, at fifty years, eleven months, and seven days, was somehow able to capture the PGA Championship in 2021 at Kiawah. Mickelson became the oldest player in the history of the sport (two and a half years older than the next oldest) to win a major. Part of Jack Nicklaus's legacy is his unforgettable win at The Masters in 1986 at the age of forty-six. Phil was nearly five years older and playing in a much more difficult era when he somehow managed to fend off Father Time for a major victory.

The Masters, as I can't seem to stop saying, is the most prestigious of all the majors. It means more at Augusta. It just does. Winning a green jacket is the height of golf. I put more value in winning there than I do winning at Chambers Bay or Olympia Fields. The player with the most wins at Augusta is Jack Nicklaus with six. Second is Tiger with five. Arnie is third with four. And guess who's tied for fourth with three? That's right, Lefty.

Phil is easily the greatest left-handed golfer to ever do it. Add up all the other major championships won by lefties—five—and Phil still has more. Most of the courses on tour were designed by righties with right-handed golfers in mind. This is not nothing. Being a left-handed golfer, as I am, is a clear disadvantage.

So Phil is the best left-handed golfer of all time, he's the oldest to ever win a major, he's third in top two finishes in majors, he's fourth in green jackets, and he won six majors during the Tiger Woods era. It's an ironclad case.

The cherry on top for Phil is that he sacrificed his reputation to save the sport. In 2022, he was the face of the newly formed

LIV Golf league funded by PIF, the sovereign wealth fund of Saudi Arabia. This new league tore apart the golf world. Most people were outraged that Lefty would put his morals aside for a huge payday. Phil was reportedly paid $200 million to join LIV. I find it hard to believe that anyone would turn down that kind of money on moral grounds, especially when you consider the fact that other entities, like the U.S. government, for example, deal with the Saudis.

Here's what I love about Phil, though. He knew what he was doing. He didn't try to run from it. This is what he told biographer Alan Shipnuck that got even more people outraged:

"They're scary motherfuckers to get involved with. We know they killed [*Washington Post* reporter and U.S. resident Jamal] Khashoggi and have a horrible record on human rights. They execute people over there for being gay. Knowing all of this, why would I even consider it? Because this is a once-in-a-lifetime opportunity to reshape how the PGA Tour operates."

Mickelson practically had to go into exile due to the public outcry once this quote became public. He even skipped The Masters in 2022. Phil was crushed for being honest. And, as much as people didn't want to hear it, he was right. Here's the rest of that quote Phil gave to Shipnuck:

"They've been able to get by with manipulative, coercive, strong-arm tactics because we, the players, had no recourse. As nice a guy as [PGA Tour commissioner Jay Monahan] comes across as, unless you have leverage, he won't do what's right. And the Saudi [Public Investment Fund] money has finally given us that leverage. I'm not sure I even want [the league that would become LIV Golf] to succeed, but just the idea of it is allowing us to get things done with the [PGA] Tour."

After just a year of LIV, the PGA Tour and commissioner Jay

Monahan capitulated. In June 2023, the PGA Tour announced a partnership with PIF, the same sovereign wealth fund of Saudi Arabia that funded LIV and made it the tour's primary corporate sponsor. The same guy who paraded around for a year on his moral high horse eventually took the money, too. The same guy who Phil said wouldn't do what you wanted unless you had leverage didn't do what Phil wanted until LIV provided the leverage. In addition to taking the Saudi money, the PGA Tour has announced future tournaments without the traditional thirty-six-hole cut, significantly higher purses, and team play events. All ideas that attracted golfers like Mickelson to LIV.

Lefty was right. He took a public flogging for the betterment of the sport. Phil's sacrifice saved the sport. He was a modern-day martyr, and his big bet on using LIV as leverage to improve the PGA Tour cashed for all of us. I think he belongs on the Mount Rushmore of golf based on the merits, but saving the sport etches it in stone.

He is the fourth-best golfer of all time.

Scott Van Pelt, ESPN

I AM NOTORIOUSLY BAD AT LISTS. LISTS OF ANY KIND. I have a hard time narrowing things down and then I inevitably forget someone or something that should be on the list. Then I feel like an idiot and wish I hadn't participated. So when Stugotz asked if I'd help with this one, I thought: SIGN ME UP!!

I appreciate his passion for the game. I especially enjoy him asking me when I come on the show if I can get him on

at Augusta. Sure, Stugotz, how's Tuesday sound? I'll get you penciled in at 10:28. Or is early afternoon preferable? The best part is I believe he's entirely serious. What a joyous dumbass.

From a notoriously shitty list maker, I'd start by saying: his list is fine. If you watch Golf Channel all day and want to go back to Old Tom and dudes playing in tweed blazers, have a ball. I'm happier to begin in the era of Jones and Sarazen. I, at least, have some understanding of their importance. There have been amazing players heavy on personality and swagger like Seve, Trevino, and Norman. Ruthless major winners like Player and Watson and Faldo. The combination of class, elegance, and brilliant play is all combined in a man like Byron Nelson as well, and he won eleven tournaments in a row. He deserves mention for that alone.

Sam Snead gets his own paragraph as a combo of a pile of wins, a stack of majors, a truly legendary swing, and the twinkle in his eye that let you know he had a punch line coming that might have been OB. If he makes your list, no issue.

To me, Tiger, Jack, and Arnie get no pushback. But clearly Phil is where Stugotz is the one with the twinkle in his eye. Is there a case? Sure. His majors, his close calls, his fuckups; I mean what else do we call Winged Foot? He called himself an idiot for eighteen on Sunday. If he finishes that off and ultimately gets the slam, the case is stronger. As an aside, I'd say this: I was there at Muirfield when he won the Open and his final round was as good as it gets. Phil's a gambler, so am I. I'd have lost all the money I had if you'd told me fifteen years ago Phil would win that major. His game didn't fit what was required. He lacked the patience to solve that riddle. Then he shot a brilliant 66 and blew my mind. It speaks to the genius of his talents. His duel with Henrik Stenson at Troon was nuts, too. Phil beat everyone on earth not named Stenson by eleven. But Henrik beat him by three. It said his game was still there at forty-six. Not bad for an old dude.

Then he got in insane shape and became the oldest major winner ever at Kiawah. I was there for that one, too. In the final group with Brooks the Badass. Outdrove him. Stared him down and didn't blink. Strong, strong stuff.

But he's not 4.

It's gotta be Hogan.

"Iconic" is the word. The swing, the hat, the scowl, the crash, the comeback. Ben Hogan is like a make-believe real-life thing. His *Five Lessons* book has to be the most-read book about the swing and is the foundation of who knows how many men and women who try to find the secret in the dirt.

The personalities of so many of the others, including Phil, are so much better known. Hogan is more a mystery. Maybe it's because I see him in that black-and-white picture on eighteen at Merion and wonder if he was as cold-blooded as described.

Story goes that he was playing with Claude Harmon in The Masters and Claude aced the twelfth. Yeah—that hole. The one you see when you close your eyes and hear that piano and Jim Nantz's voice. Made a 1.

Hogan says nothing. No reaction. Walks over the bridge . . . nada. Harmon takes the ball out, gives a wave to the roars from the patrons. Hogan then makes a birdie.

As they walk to thirteen, Hogan says, "Claude, I can't remember the last time I made a two there. What did you make?"

C'mon.

Nine majors, one of five to complete the Slam, the swing, the aura . . . Hogan rounds out my foursome.

But, again, lists are not my strength. Neither is getting tee times at Augusta, buddy. Love you.

The Rebuttal to the Rebuttal

So, 10:04 next Saturday? I'll meet you on Magnolia Lane.

16

THE COMPILER

CLOSE YOUR EYES. NOW I WANT YOU TO THINK OF A GREAT athlete. Any athlete. But a great athlete. OK, do you have someone in mind? You do? Good. Now I want you to think about what, in your mind, elevated them to the level of great. Was it their dominance on the field, court, or ice? Or was it how long they played their respective sport? If you have half a brain, like I do, then the answer was dominance.

Playing for fifteen-plus seasons does not make someone one of the best. Yes, it's hard to last that long in professional sports. Hell, it's hard to last that long in anything. That kind of longevity is impressive, but it does not automatically elevate someone to the elite of the elite. Le Batard and I have been doing radio for damn near twenty years and we're not in the Radio Hall of Fame. Yet. We should be, honestly. And we will be. To be considered one of the best you have to stand out among your peers in your sport and/or at your position. You can't just have hung around the longest.

Ask yourself this. Who was a better running back: Barry Sanders or Frank Gore? Gore was trying to run his way to the Hall of Fame three yards at a time as recently as 2022, but it's Sanders. Who was a better wide receiver: Calvin Johnson or Keenan McCardell? Megatron. Which was the better band: Nirvana or Electric Light Orchestra? Smells like Nirvana. Who was the better actor: Heath Ledger or Kevin Costner? *Dances with Wolves* sucked. It's Ledger in a rout.

The Jacksonville Jaguars drafted Tony Boselli out of USC with the second pick of the 1995 draft. It was the first pick in the history of the Jaguars, one of the two expansion teams that year, along with the Carolina Panthers. The offensive tackle was taken to be the cornerstone of the franchise. And he was. Boselli was a day-one starter at a premier position in the NFL and protected Jaguar quarterbacks like the Secret Service protects the president.

Boselli was voted to the Pro Bowl five straight years from 1996 to 2000. He was named as a first-team All-Pro in 1997, 1998, and 1999. Boselli was so dominant that he was named to the 1990s All-Decade Team (second team), which was decided on by the Pro Football Hall of Fame. That means he was universally recognized as one of the top four offensive tackles of the entire decade. A decade in which he did not enter the NFL until it was halfway through.

Boselli's stalwart play at left tackle coincided with a string of success previously unheard of for an expansion team. The

Jaguars made it to the AFC Championship Game in just their second season. They went 11–5 in each of their next two seasons, advancing to the divisional round in one of them. Then, in 1999, Jacksonville went 14–2 and earned the #1 seed in the AFC, culminating in another trip to the AFC Championship Game.

Tony Boselli was the anchor of those successful Jaguar teams. He cleared lanes for running back Fred Taylor and kept quarterback Mark Brunell upright. Boselli was also a fan favorite in the community. So much so that in 1998 McDonald's unveiled the "Boselli Burger." The burger featured three patties, lettuce, and tomatoes and was placed on the kind of buns used for the McRib. A massive sandwich befitting of the massive man it was named in honor of.

CRAIG BIGGIO WAS FAR from massive. He was listed at 5-foot-11, so he was probably actually 5-9. The Houston Astros drafted the scrappy, diminutive catcher out of Seton Hall in the first round of the 1987 Draft. Biggio made it to The Show in 1988 and after a few seasons behind the plate he moved to second base, where he played for the rest of his career. Despite his quick ascent to the Major Leagues, he was not an overnight sensation. In his first four years in the league, he averaged seven home runs and forty-eight runs batted in per season.

During Biggio's third full season in the bigs, the Astros brought up a new first baseman: Jeff Bagwell. Bagwell knocked in eighty-two runs en route to Rookie of the Year honors. He would be named as the National League's Most Valuable Player three years later. The Astros had the right side of their infield set for the next fifteen years, but the team still stunk. Houston failed to make the playoffs in each of Biggio's first nine seasons.

IN 2002, THE NEWLY formed Houston Texans selected Tony Boselli first overall in the expansion draft. Every team in the league had to put five players on a list for the Texans to choose from. The Jaguars were in salary cap hell, so they put Boselli and his nearly $7 million cap hit on the list. It was fitting for the first draft pick in the history of the Jaguars to become the first expansion draft pick in the history of the Houston Texans, but Boselli never played a down for Houston. A left shoulder injury forced him to retire at the age of thirty-one.

The injury happened, according to Boselli, sometime during the 1998 season, but he played through the pain. After years of fighting through the discomfort of his banged-up shoulder he finally opted for surgery, and things didn't go according to plan. Boselli's shoulder was completely shot. An incredible career cut short because of a lingering injury and a botched surgery.

BIGGIO JUST KEPT PLAYING. He played in 150 or more games in eleven seasons. He led the Major Leagues in plate appearances five times. The guy was durable. Some say availability is the best ability. Sure, it helps, but I think talent is a much better ability than availability. I mean, I'd rather have a superstar athlete who misses a lot of games like Joel Embiid than a guy who shows up every night but is a stiff like Mason Plumlee.

Biggio was selected to the All-Star Team for five straight

years (1994–98). In that stretch, the Astros made the playoffs twice and lost in the first round each time. The last year Biggio made the All-Star Team was 1998, but he played for nine more seasons after that.

The Astros finally won a playoff series in 2004, when Biggio was thirty-eight years old. By that time Lance Berkman and Carlos Beltrán were carrying the offense and Roy Oswalt, Roger Clemens—The Rocket, and Andy Pettitte were mystifying opposing hitters. Houston made it to the World Series in 2005, but they were swept by the Chicago White Sox in what has to be the least memorable Fall Classic of my lifetime.

By that point, Biggio was a shell of himself defensively. He was no longer stealing many bases and his batting average was declining. Surprisingly, though, his home run numbers were up. Now, I'm not saying that Craig Biggio took steroids or any other performance-enhancing drug. All I'm saying is that his best three-year stretch in terms of home runs came when he was between the ages of thirty-eight and forty. That's all I'm saying. If you're hearing something else, that's *you* saying it.

BY ANY METRIC, TONY Boselli is a Hall of Famer. Five straight Pro Bowls. First Team All-Pro three straight times. Named to the All-Decade Team.

Did he dominate? Check.

Did he contribute to winning? He was an integral piece of an expansion team that went to the playoffs four straight years and to two AFC Championship Games. Check.

The only knock against him was that he played only ninety-one games. But guess what? Hall of Famers Doak Walker (sixty-seven), Gale Sayers (sixty-eight), Terrell Davis (seventy-eight),

Steve Van Buren (eighty-three), Kenny Easley (eighty-nine), and twenty-one others all played fewer.

Boselli was a Hall of Fame finalist in 2017, 2018, 2019, 2020, and 2021, and didn't get in.

ON JUNE 28, 2007, Craig Biggio recorded his 3,000th career hit. A certifiable ticket to the Hall of Fame. A month later he announced that he would retire at the end of the season. He was forty-one years old. In 2015, his third year on the ballot, he was voted into the Baseball Hall of Fame.

Craig Biggio was a very good baseball player. But was he great? His entire Hall of Fame case is based on his longevity. He's twenty-fifth all time in hits, but he's also eleventh all time in plate appearances. No second baseman has played as many games and no second baseman has had as many at bats.

Throw out his four Gold Gloves, because we all know they're a popularity contest. Biggio was a below-average second baseman defensively. Offensively, he hit a lot of doubles, but his career .281 batting average puts him fifteenth among the twenty second basemen in the Hall of Fame. The stat where he stands out the most is being hit by pitches. He was plunked 285 times in his career. Only Hughie Jennings, who was born in 1869, was beaned more (287). Hustling Hughie! Eh-Yah!

Did Craig Biggio lead to winning? No. During his individual peak the Astros won one playoff game and lost six. In fact, they didn't win a playoff series until his seventeenth season with the team. They made the playoffs only six times in his twenty years with the club. And on the rare occasion that Biggio's teams did make it, he was less of a player. He was a career .234 hitter in the postseason.

Find me a statistical argument without using counting stats that makes the case for Biggio to be in the Hall of Fame. Go ahead. I dare you. He's a compiler. In fact, I'm removing Biggio from the Baseball Hall of Fame and inducting him into the Compilers Hall of Fame on the first ballot.

TONY BOSELLI WASN'T A compiler. He was one of the elite physical forces in a league filled with physical freaks. And after years of tireless campaigning and lobbying by me, Boselli finally got his gold jacket in 2022. I was there for everything: the parade, the induction, the speech.

Now listen. Did I cozy up to Boselli and spearhead his Hall of Fame push solely because he's my fallback plan once Le Batard and I eventually break up? Yes, but Boselli deserved it. That guy was great. I mean, he's so good at blocking that I never got within ten feet of him until he put his guard down after the ceremony.

So Biggio is out. Boselli is in. And I'm right where I'm at my best—nestled up close to someone more famous than me who provides the kind of credibility I could never have on my own.

Boselli and Stu coming your way live from 4 to 7 P.M. on Jacksonville's #1 sports talk station. We'll take your calls at 1-800-CANTON and we'll both be wearing gold jackets.

Tony Boselli, Pro Football Hall of Famer

BACK IN 2019 STUGOTZ TOLD ME THAT HE WAS GOING TO start a campaign to get me inducted into the Pro Football Hall of Fame. From what I can tell, all he ever did was tell me

about all the stuff he was going to do. According to Stugotz, there were going to be a whole host of interviews with Hall of Fame defensive linemen whom I played against. There was going to be an online petition. He was going to talk to as many people from the Hall of Fame selection committee as he could. He even mentioned how he was going to put up a billboard in Canton. None of it happened.

I was really never counting on Stugotz to do anything he said, and thankfully I was fortunate enough to be inducted into the Hall in August 2022. A week before the ceremony, Stugotz called and asked if he could attend the festivities. He kept saying, "We did it, Tony," as if he had anything to do with it. I told him that he was more than welcome to come to Canton. After all, Stugotz was always my backup plan when it came to my career in sports media.

Outside of asking to wear the gold jacket upward of twenty times, Stugotz was fine in Canton. There were plenty of other Hall of Famers whom he tried to cozy up next to, so for the most part he kept a safe distance from my family. However, in typical Stugotz fashion, by the end of the weekend he had somehow become friends with my golfing buddies and got himself invited to come up and hang out in Ponte Vedra, which he promised to do, but, as expected, he has never shown up.

I have hardly heard from Stugotz since my induction weekend until this odd request to chime in on his book appeared. I'm sure he thinks that this chapter is proof that he was, in fact, trying to get a campaign started to get me into the Hall.

Either way, Craig Biggio was ten times better at baseball than Stugotz ever was at radio.

17

THE TRUTH WILL SET YOU SPREE

I'M NOT A STATS GUY. I'M MORE OF A GUT GUY. A SMELL-TEST guy. An eye-test guy. But sometimes, even I rub my belly, take a whiff, and look at numbers.

I don't normally recommend this, but give it a try. Just this once.

Which player do you think had a better career?

Player A—18.2 points, 3 rebounds, 3 assists, five-time All-Star, never made first- or second-team All-NBA, never made an All-Defensive Team.

Player B—18.3 points, 4.1 rebounds, 4 assists, four-time All-Star, first-team All-NBA (one time), second-team All-Defensive (one time).

Player A is Reggie Miller. Player B is Latrell Sprewell.

Miller is in the Basketball Hall of Fame and was named as one of the league's Top 75 players of all time. Sprewell is far from both.

Look at those numbers again. Something doesn't add up.

Miller took on the role of villain in seven playoff series against the New York Knicks throughout the '90s and stayed relevant by becoming a broadcaster. Voilà—Hall of Famer.

His defining moment came in 1995 when he scored eight points in nine seconds to steal Game 1 of the Eastern Conference Semis against the Knicks. Miller's Indiana Pacers ultimately won that series, but got bounced by the Orlando Magic in the next round. He has ridden the praise from that game all the way to the Hall of Fame. When people think about Reggie Miller, they think about three-point shooting and how he went back and forth with Spike Lee in Madison Square Garden. That's it. They don't think about winning, because he didn't do much of it that mattered.

Sure, Reggie talked a lot of trash, but so would I if I had Dale and Antonio Davis protecting me everywhere I went. Not to mention Rik Smits—The Dunking Dutchman—operating out of the post and New York's own Mark Jackson setting him up for open shots. The Pacers were a well-oiled machine orchestrated by Larry Brown and then Larry Bird, and Miller was nothing more than a cog in it. He got all the media coverage simply because he was the squeaky wheel.

He portrayed himself as the villain, but in reality he was a choker. He went 3–18 in the decisive Game 6 against the eighth-seeded Knicks in the 1999 Eastern Conference Finals. Then, the one time the Pacers made it to the NBA Finals, Miller went 1 for 16 from the floor in Game 1 against the Lakers. Honestly, forget about the eight points in nine seconds. The playoff moment that truly defines his career came in 2004, when Tayshaun Prince of the Detroit Pistons chased him down and blocked his layup attempt in the Eastern Conference Finals.

FOR SPREWELL, PLAYING THE villain, or the choker, was not an act. In 1993, he fought with teammate Byron Houston, who had him by fifty pounds and gave off serious Mike Tyson vibes. In 1995, he went at it with teammate Jerome Kersey and then returned to practice carrying a two-by-four and reportedly threatened to come back the next time with a gun. His defining moment came in 1997, when he attacked head coach P. J. Carlesimo during a practice and choked him for nearly ten seconds before teammates and assistant coaches could step in. Sprewell left practice, showered, and then charged at Carlesimo again, this time landing a blow on his right cheek. The league suspended him for sixty-eight games, but he got new life after the lockout in '99 with the Knicks.

Sprewell came off the bench and was the sparkplug the Knicks needed as the eighth seed in the Eastern Conference. New York knocked off the top-seeded Miami Heat, the Cleveland Cavaliers, and Reggie Miller and the Pacers on the way to the NBA Finals. The Spurs took care of the Knicks in five games, but Sprewell elevated his game on the grandest stage, averaging twenty-six a night in the Finals.

REGGIE MILLER IS THOUGHT of as one of the all-time greats, but I'd take Spree over him every day of the week and twice on Sunday. Hell, Reggie Miller isn't even the best basketball player in his own family. His sister Cheryl was named the Naismith Player of the Year three times, won two NCAA titles, and led Team USA to the gold medal in 1984.

Not only that, but Reggie doesn't even make my All-Miller Starting Five:

PG—Andre Miller
SG—Mike Miller
SF—Cheryl Miller
PF—Oliver Miller
C—Brad Miller
Sixth Man—Brandon Miller

And don't think for a second that I'm letting that fraud Sean Miller coach this team. No one has wasted more talent and sweat through more shirts in the NCAA Tournament than that guy. The coaching job, of course, goes to former Knicks interim head coach Mike Miller.

Reggie Miller never won a ring, so I can't take one away, but he was named to the NBA's Top 75 team. I am officially removing him from the list, which, because of a tie in voting, actually had seventy-six members. Reggie is out. I've taken away his sport coat with the "NBA 75" logo on it. And the Top 75 now has seventy-five members. You're welcome, Adam Silver.

18

REPLAY

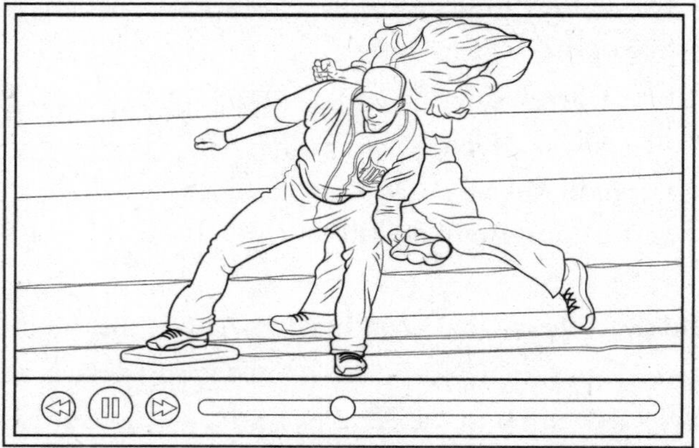

THEY SAY A PICTURE IS WORTH A THOUSAND WORDS. WHO'S "they," you ask? You know, people. Calm down. And if what they say is true, then why aren't there way more pictures in this book? And if a picture is worth a thousand words, then what's a video worth? To me, everything.

Twenty-seven up. Twenty-seven down. Baseball immortality. There have been over three hundred no-hitters in Major League Baseball history, but only twenty-three of them have been perfect. No hits. No walks. No errors. No base runners. Perfect. Only twenty-three pitchers have done it. That's it. Twice as many people have been president of the United States.

Some of the all-time greats have achieved perfection. Cy Young. Sandy Koufax. Don Larsen for the Yankees in the World Series against the Dodgers in 1956. Jim "Catfish" Hunter. Randy

Johnson—The Big Unit. David Wells the morning after a bender with a massive hangover. David Cone. Roy Halladay.

On June 2, 2010, Detroit Tigers pitcher Armando Galarraga was moments away from joining that exclusive club. The Tigers led the Cleveland Indians 3–0 in the top half of the ninth inning. Galarraga had retired the first twenty-six batters that he faced. The twenty-seventh batter was Indians shortstop Jason Donald. On the third pitch of the at bat Donald hit a soft ground ball to the first-base side. Tigers first baseman Miguel Cabrera—Miggy—fielded it cleanly and threw it to Galarraga covering the bag. It was a bang-bang play and first-base umpire Jim Joyce called Donald safe. The bid for the perfect game was over.

After watching one replay it was clear that Joyce's vision was worse than the Irish novelist whose name he shares. Galarraga had control of the ball and his foot clearly touched first base before Donald's did. Couldn't be any clearer. Go watch it. It's not even close. Joyce blew it. He botched what should have been a perfect game. After the game he fought back tears as he acknowledged his mistake. When asked about Joyce's blown call, Galarraga replied, "Nobody's perfect."

Well, Galarraga was perfect that day and his name has been erased from all the history books, except this one, because of a fifty-five-year-old umpire's deteriorating vision and Major League Baseball's aversion to adaptation. Stodgy old baseball was the last of the four major North American professional sports to institute an instant replay review system. It wasn't until 2014 that plays on the basepaths became reviewable. They had the technology for years, but because they're enamored with the past and reluctant to change, they didn't use it. Major League Baseball should be ashamed of itself.

The pitch that induced Donald's ground ball to the right

side was just the eighty-third thrown by Galarraga that day. Had Joyce made the right call it would have been the second-most efficient perfect game in MLB history. Only Addie Joss—The Human Hairpin—of the Cleveland Naps back in October 1908 retired all twenty-seven batters in fewer pitches (seventy-four).

Jim Joyce better write me a fat check, because I am now doing what MLB should have done back in 2010: officially correcting his egregious mistake and granting him peace of mind. Jason Donald was out at first base. The game ended right then and there. Armando Galarraga threw a perfect game. So let it be written. So let it be done.

THERE'S SOMETHING ABOUT HIGH-LEVERAGE plays at first base that is difficult for the men in blue because I have another obvious error to correct. Game 6 of the 1985 World Series. The St. Louis Cardinals led the series three games to two and took a 1–0 lead over the Kansas City Royals into the bottom of the ninth. The Cards were just three outs away from winning their tenth World Series in franchise history.

Pinch hitter Jorge Orta led off the final frame for the Royals and bounced a ground ball to the right side. Jack Clark fielded it cleanly and flipped it to pitcher Todd Worrell covering first base. Worrell caught the toss and touched first base before Orta—again, clear as day, but first-base umpire Don Denkinger ruled Orta safe.

Cardinals manager Whitey Herzog was apoplectic. Denkinger, who was also the crew chief, refused to change the call. The Royals scored two runs in the inning to win Game 6, and then blasted the Cards 10–0 in Game 7 to win the World Series.

As the great Lee Corso would say, "Not so fast, my friend."

The game and the Series turned because of an egomaniacal umpire's blunder. Orta was definitely out at first base. That's out number one. Out number two is for Denkinger's defiance and baseball's having the technology to clear it up but refusing to use it. And out number three is for Kansas City fans getting to enjoy Patrick Mahomes light up the NFL, while I'm stuck with the Jets. The 1985 Royals are now stripped of their rings. George Brett never won a World Series and neither did future Met Bret Saberhagen. The St. Louis Cardinals are your 1985 World Series champions. Congratulate them.

HALL OF FAME PITCHER Lefty Gomez once said he'd rather be lucky than good. And that's what the Colorado Buffaloes football team was in 1990. Lucky. In their fifth game of the year, they trailed Missouri 31–27 late in the fourth quarter, but they had the ball in the red zone. With under a minute to play, Colorado quarterback Charles Johnson completed a pass to tight end Jon Boman, who fell down shy of the end zone at the 3-yard line. Johnson hurried the offense to the line and on first down he spiked the ball to stop the clock with twenty-eight ticks remaining. On second down Johnson handed the ball off to running back Eric Bieniemy, who was stopped short of the goal line. Colorado called their final time-out with eighteen seconds left.

On third down they handed it to Bieniemy again. And again he was stopped just short of the goal line. The clock continued to tick away, but then it was paused briefly by the referees for reasons that remain unclear as they untangled the pile at the goal line. With the clock again counting down, Johnson hurried the offense to the line. On fourth down, he spiked the ball with two seconds left. It should have been a turnover on downs and

Missouri's ball. Instead, on what was essentially Colorado's fifth down, Johnson called his own number and broke the plane for a touchdown. The Buffaloes won the game, 33–31.

Colorado finished the season 11–1–1 and ranked #1 in the AP poll. Georgia Tech went 11–0–1 and was ranked #1 in the Coaches Poll. They shared the national title . . . until now. Colorado has been lucky that no one has stripped them of this bogus national title claim, but that luck stops right here. Right now. No rings. Colorado lost to Missouri and finished 10–2–1. Georgia Tech won the national championship outright.

WAS BRETT HULL IN the crease when he scored the game-winning goal for the Dallas Stars in Game 6 of the 1999 Stanley Cup Finals? Yes, but I can't assume that the Buffalo Sabres would have won Game 6 and then gone on to win Game 7. Actually, you know what? Screw it. The Sabres won the Cup in '99. Jump through some folding tables, Buffalo fans.

Did the refs and the Russkies cheat in the 1972 gold medal men's basketball game? Absolutely. The United States has now won the gold, just like we won the Cold War.

Are there five or six other famous calls in sports history that you want me to overturn? There are? Good. Send them to me. I'll put them in the paperback, and we can split the profits. 90–10 my way.

19

PARADE OF SADNESS

RAY BOURQUE PLAYED FOR THE BOSTON BRUINS FOR MORE than two decades. Throughout the 1980s and '90s he was one of the best, if not the best, defensemen in the NHL. He won the Norris Trophy, given annually to the best defenseman in the league, five times. Twice he finished second for the Hart Trophy, the regular-season MVP Award. And both times he lost to a member of the Edmonton Oilers. In 1987 he was beaten out by Wayne Gretzky—The Great One. In 1990, he finished second to Mark Messier—The Messiah.

Twice Bourque led the Bruins to the Stanley Cup Final. And both times they lost to the Edmonton Oilers. In 1988 they were swept by the Oilers, who were captained by Wayne Gretzky—The Great One. In 1990, the Bruins lost in five to an Edmonton team captained by Mark Messier—The Messiah.

I think there might be a pattern there.

Boston made it to the Eastern Conference Finals in '91 and '92, but their championship window was closing and it was closing fast. In 1997, the Bruins' record streak of twenty-nine straight playoff berths was snapped. Three years later the B's were stuck in last place and Bourque, their captain, chose not to go down with the ship. He demanded a trade, and in early March 2000 he was sent to the Colorado Avalanche.

The Avs team he joined was loaded. They had won the Cup in 1996 and had reached the Conference Finals in both '97 and '99. They had Joe Sakic, Peter Forsberg, Milan Hejduk, Chris Drury, and Patrick Roy, one of the best goalies in the history of the NHL even though he mispronounced his own last name. With Bourque on board they made it back to the Western Conference Finals in 2000, but lost in seven games to the Dallas Stars.

The following year the stars aligned. The Avalanche plowed through the regular season, amassing a league-best 118 points. In the postseason they swept the Canucks, snuck by the Kings, belted the Blues, and skated past the Devils in seven games to win the Cup. Avalanche captain Joe Sakic broke with tradition and handed the Cup to Bourque out of respect so that the future Hall of Famer could be the first one to skate around the ice while hoisting Lord Stanley's Cup.

WADE BOGGS WAS A natural-born hitter. The third baseman walked into Major League Baseball with the Boston Red Sox in 1982 and started raking. He hit .325 or better in his first eight seasons in the league and collected five batting titles in the process.

Boggs also had a great eye at the plate, and he rarely struck out. He led the league in walks on two separate occasions and never struck out more than seventy times in any of his eighteen seasons in the league. Mike Trout, arguably the best hitter of the modern era, has struck out more than seventy times in every season of his career. If Trout ever wins a playoff game, it will be his first. Do it in the playoffs, Trout. Seriously. If you're so great you'd show up in October. Trout. What a bum. That wasn't nice, but you know what is? Boggs still holds the record for batting average at Fenway Park at .369.

His prowess at the plate was nothing new for Boston fans. He was just the next Hall of Fame hitter from the left side for the Red Sox. First it was Ted Williams, the Splendid Splinter. Then it was Carl Yastrzemski, Yaz. After Yaz came Wade Boggs. And after Boggs was David Ortiz, Big Papi.

THE MOUNT RUSHMORE OF LEFT-HANDED HITTERS IN RED SOX HISTORY

Teddy Ballgame
Yaz
Wade Boggs
Big Papi
Troy O'Leary
Tris Speaker
Trot Nixon
Bill Buckner

The Red Sox missed the playoffs in each of Boggs's first four seasons with the club. In 1986, they were one strike away from winning the World Series, but my dad prematurely opened that bottle of champagne and the Mets rallied to win Games 6 and 7. Boston won the division in 1988 and 1990 but were swept by the Oakland Athletics in the ALCS both times. They missed the postseason altogether in '91 and '92.

Boggs was a free agent following the 1992 season, and after eleven seasons in Boston, he decided to sign with the New York Yankees. Yes, the Red Sox and Yankees were bitter rivals. Decades of animosity had been built up between the fan bases. But the Yankees of the '80s and early '90s were not the evil empire they would become in the mid- to late '90s. In 1992, they were bottom-feeders. New York had not made the postseason since 1981. Boggs wasn't even in the league back then. The Yankees were coming off four straight losing seasons when he joined them.

With Boggs at the hot corner, the Yankees started The Climb. They missed the playoffs in '93. In '94 they were in first place, but the strike ended the season abruptly. In '95 they made it to the playoffs, but lost to the Ken Griffey, Jr.–led Seattle Mariners in an epic five-game Division Series. In 1996, in Boggs's fourth full season in pinstripes, the Yankees beat the Braves in six games to win the World Series.

IN JUNE 2001, BOSTON sports fans were desperate for a winner. The Patriots were coming off a 5–11 season and had just drafted Tom Brady in the sixth round. The Celtics had just doused themselves in garlic to ward off the three-hundred-year-old vampire they had coaching them the past three and a half seasons in Rick Pitino. The Red Sox hadn't won the World Series since 1918 and had just missed the playoffs in 2000. And the Bruins were coming off back-to-back seasons without a postseason berth and hadn't won the Cup since 1972.

The city was so starved for a successful sports story that just three days after Ray Bourque finally got his paws on the Stanley Cup, they threw him a rally. Please remember that he won the Cup with Colorado. I wish I were making this up. Fans from all over New England flocked to City Hall Plaza to celebrate the Avalanche's title. Police estimated the crowd to be north of fifteen thousand truly pathetic people. The city of Boston should be ashamed of itself. A massive crowd of New Englanders came out to vicariously celebrate a title that was won by a team from Colorado. If you were celebrating at City Hall Plaza that day and you're reading this, I hate you.

During that rally, Bourque told the crowd of losers that he will always be a member of the Boston Bruins, so I'm going to take him at his word. Ray Bourque was never traded to the Avalanche and his name has officially been erased from Lord Stanley's Cup. Listen up, Bourque. Demanding a trade because you yourself are not good enough to win the Stanley Cup on your own team and joining a team that was right on the cusp? Smells like Durant. Didn't let him get away with it either. You can't do it. It's as simple as that.

And, Joe Sakic, what are you doing? You earned that Stanley Cup. You led that team. You didn't request a trade. You stayed put. You stayed with your guys. And you not skating around the ice with the Stanley Cup first, as tradition dictates, was wrong. You handed it to a guy who took a shortcut, rode your coattails, and got the credit that you deserved. You know what, Sakic? Or should I call you just "ic" because you didn't have the Sak to do what you should have? I'm taking a Cup away from you, too. It's gone.

WADE BOGGS PLAYED FOR the Yankees again in 1997, but their title defense came up short as they were bounced in the ALDS by the Cleveland Indians. The following year Boggs continued his tour of AL East teams and signed with the Tampa Bay Devil Rays. It was a bit of a homecoming for him, too. Boggs's family moved to Tampa when he was eleven, and he had gone to high school there. Tampa finished in last place in both of his seasons there and failed to win seventy games in either of them, but Boggs was a solid veteran. He hit .301 in his final season and became the first player in the history of Major League Baseball to hit a home run for his 3,000th career hit.

Boggs was a colorful character both on and off the field. He routinely drank fifty to sixty beers during cross-country flights, guest-starred on the popular television shows of his time (*Cheers, Seinfeld, The Simpsons*), and like many baseball players was superstitious. He woke up at the same time every day, ate chicken before every game, and wrote the word "chai" in the dirt of the batter's box before every at bat. "Chai" is a Hebrew word that means "life." Boggs is not Jewish. I am. And I did not know that. Wade Boggs is more Jewish than I am. In fact, he's now among my top 5 of the best Jewish athletes of all time.

TOP 5 JEWISH ATHLETES OF ALL TIME

OLI

Sid Luckman
Shawn Green

Ryan Braun, The Hebrew Hammer
Sue Bird
Mark Spitz
Hank Greenberg, Hammerin' Hank

5. Wade Boggs
4. Anthony Schwartz
3. JuJu Smith-Schuster
2. Tarik Cohen
1. Sandy Koufax

L'Chaim.

Perhaps the most public display of his colorful personality came amid the on-field frenzy after winning the World Series in 1996. Boggs, for some reason, mounted a police horse and did a victory lap around Yankee Stadium with his index finger pointed to the sky. Unlike Bourque, Boggs didn't go celebrate his championship with Boston. Or their lame fans. Nor did he do it in Tampa Bay with Dick Vitale. He has a strong case as it is, but for that and that alone, Wade Boggs, you keep your ring.

Bob Ryan, *Boston Globe* columnist

YES, THE LOCALS HERE IN BOSTON ACTUALLY WELCOMED back Ray Bourque so he could display the Stanley Cup he had just helped his team win.

Make that another team.

Who does that?

I'll tell you when that happens. You do that when the person in question is totally beloved. He had given his all to the

Boston Bruins from 1979–80 to late in the 1999–2000 season, when he was allowed an escape to the Colorado Avalanche. No one complained. People got it. It wasn't "Don't let the door hit you in the ass." No, it was "Godspeed, Raymond."

So he goes to Colorado and gives them all eighty games. His numbers aren't dazzling (7-52-59), but you don't measure the contributions and presence of a player such as Ray Bourque in numbers alone. Besides, he's a defenseman, one with five Norris Trophies and thirteen first-team All-Star selections. You think there weren't plenty of Avalanche players who didn't learn important things just by being around Ray Bourque for a season?

And the Avalanche did win ten more games with Bourque in the lineup than they had the year before. Gee, I wonder if there was any connection.

So to argue that Ray Bourque didn't deserve his ring because he joined a "loaded" team is beyond preposterous. The truth could very well be the opposite: perhaps Ray Bourque was Colorado's missing ingredient.

People in Boston were happy for Ray Bourque, and appropriately so.

As for Wade Boggs, I really don't think enough people in Boston fully appreciated having a guy who could routinely get on base three hundred times a season and who had vastly improved as a third baseman after a somewhat rocky start. The Yankees were lucky to have him.

Of course he deserved his ring. But was he the "difference"? Not really. It just so happens the year he got his ring (1996) was the year a young shortstop named Derek Jeter was the Rookie of the Year. Just sayin'.

20

MALPRACTICE

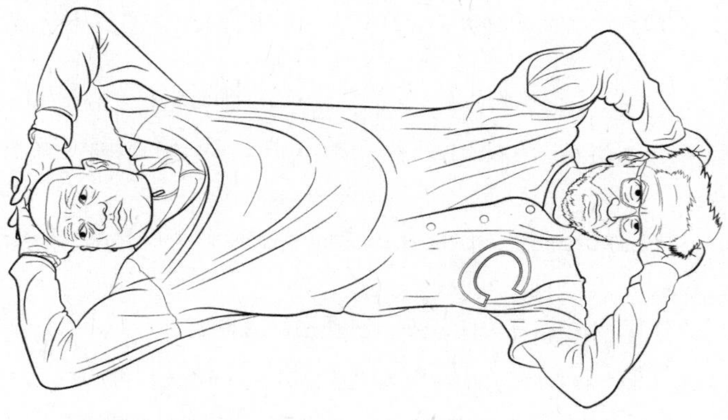

It's the middle of the night. The TV is on, the guy watching it is asleep on the couch. A commercial begins:

WHAT IF I TOLD you that two coaches, thought of as all-time greats, weren't so great at all.

That they had everyone fooled for decades.
That they each started their careers in Florida.
That one was quirky.
That one was named Glenn.
That he wasn't the quirky one.
That one lost his voice in the '90s and never got it back.
That that was Glenn.

That the other's name was Joe.

That a minor blip of success got them both a lot of undue attention.

That they loved the attention and wanted more.

That Joe hired a magician.

That the Magic made Glenn disappear.

That even without a voice, he still became a broadcaster.

THAT BOTH COACHES WOULD end up with a historic franchise.

That those historic franchises were ready-made for success.

That both would win a championship.

That I could have coached either team to those titles.

That it was the front offices that did all the work.

That neither coach deserved any of the credit.

That both were frauds and couldn't do it again.

That despite ending a franchise's 107-year championship drought, Joe was not offered a second contract.

That it was the right move.

THAT BOTH WENT TO Los Angeles.

That each would be handed another loaded roster.

That neither would ever return to the semifinals.

That Glenn's former team has been to the semis six times since he left.

That one traded for his son.

That the son lived up to the family name.

By never living up to the expectations.

That one couldn't get to the playoffs with the top two players in the sport.

That the best he could do was fourth in the AL West.

That Ranker.com thinks he's the twentieth best manager in the history of baseball.

That Glenn couldn't get it done in Philly, either.

That he lost in a Game 7 ten different times.

That Game 7s oftentimes come down to coaching.

That the NBA still named him as a Top 15 coach of all time.

THAT WE SHOULD HAVE known better.

That having six straight losing seasons in the minors was telling.

That bringing mimes and snakes to the clubhouse does not make you a good manager.

That Joe only wore dark-rimmed glasses to appear smarter than he was.

That he has 20-20 vision.

THAT GLENN'S NICKNAME IS Doc.

That Doc couldn't diagnose a defense.

That Doc was so bad in Philly that they replaced him with a Nurse.

That no one has done less with more.

THAT I WOULD HAVE coached the Celtics and Cubs to multiple championships.

That I'm taking away their rings.

That I'm giving those rings to Theo Epstein and Danny Ainge.

That neither Doc nor Joe will ever get into Cooperstown or Springfield . . . without a ticket.

ESPN Films Presents . . . *Malpractice*. A 30 for 30 about how the greatest trick that Joe Maddon and Doc Rivers ever pulled was convincing the public that they were good coaches.

21

HOUSTON, WE HAVE NO PROBLEMS

ONE OF MY FAVORITE CARD GAMES IS CALLED BULLSHIT. IT'S a simple game for three or more people where the goal is to get rid of all the cards in your hand. Whoever starts the game places as many aces as they have face down and announces the total. "Two aces," for example. The person next to them puts down all their twos. "One two." And so on. But you can lie. If you don't have any threes and it's your turn you just have to bluff your way through it. If someone suspects you of lying, they can call "Bullshit" and flip over the card(s) you put down. If you're lying, you have to pick up the entire pile. If you're being truthful, the person who called "Bullshit" on you has to pick up the pile.

Years ago, after I'd won my third game in a row, I told my dad one of my many tricks. If it was my turn to put down jacks and I had three of them, I would say "Three jacks" and actually put down four or five cards. If someone called "Bullshit" they'd turn over the three jacks and be forced to pick up the entire pile. I was just padding my truth with a few extra cards.

"You can't do that!" I remember my dad exclaiming.

"Of course I can, Dad," I replied. "The name of the game is Bullshit."

A couple of weeks later my mom told me that he was caught throwing cards on the ground. I've never been prouder of him.

THE HOUSTON ASTROS CHEATED their way to the World Series title in 2017. They used a center field camera to steal signs from opposing catchers. They relayed this stolen information to their hitters in the batter's box by banging on a trash can to indicate when an off-speed pitch was coming. It was a simple and pretty brilliant scheme. They would have gotten away with it, too, but Mike Fiers, a relief pitcher on the title-winning team, gave up the game to Ken Rosenthal of *The Athletic* in November 2019.

Major League Baseball's investigation confirmed the scheme, but commissioner Rob Manfred didn't have the stones to vacate the championship. He said he was concerned about the precedent it would set. Manfred. What a joke. Letting the Astros keep the title was wrong. And this book is all about righting the wrongs in sports. I took that title and all the rings away just like that in 2019, right after the story came out.

I even gave Houston second baseman José Altuve's MVP to Yankees outfielder Aaron Judge. Altuve hit a walk-off home run in Game 6 of the American League Championship Series off Yankee closer Aroldis Chapman to send Houston to the World Series. As he rounded third base, Altuve pointed to his jersey, seemingly suggesting to his teammates not to rip it off in celebration. Many speculated that he was wearing some sort of buzzer that let him know that Chapman was going to throw the slider that he mashed to left-center.

Instead of vacating anything, Manfred suspended Astros GM Jeff Luhnow, manager A. J. Hinch, and former bench coach Alex Cora, who at that point was the manager of the Red Sox, for a year. He docked the team some draft picks and fined them $5 million. As for the players, who the investigation confirmed were the driving force of the scheme, nothing. No punishment. No acknowledgment of wrongdoing. No apology. Nothing. Manfred even went out of his way to protect them. The following season he sent a memo to teams warning them that if they threw at Astros hitters they would be punished.

The only player from the 2017 team who was affected at all was Carlos Beltrán, who, in the wake of the scandal, resigned as the manager of the New York Mets before he ever managed a game. I hate them.

With Hinch fired and suspended, the Astros turned to Dusty Baker to rebuild the culture. Baker had been a manager for more than twenty years but had never led a team to a title. He was a safe choice. Put there to restore order and navigate some turbulent waters. His job was to stem the tide and hopefully keep the team competitive.

TOP 5 ATHLETES AND ENTERTAINERS WHO CONNOTE A PROFESSION

OLI

Dusty Baker
Gardner Minshew

Nick Nurse
Karl Malone, The Mailman
Ron Artest
Sgt. Slaughter
Matt Painter
John Clayton, The Professor
Chris Carpenter

5. Secretariat
4. Anthony Mason
3. Tiki Barber
2. Dr. J
1. Lawyer Milloy

The Astros immediately became the villains of Major League Baseball. Other fan bases hated them for cheating their way to a ring. They hated them more than the Yankee teams of the late '90s who spent their way to rings. The A in Astros was like the scarlet letter of Hester Prynne. The Astros had been branded as the enemy. Everyone was rooting against them.

When MLB returned in 2021, the Astros were without George Springer, Justin Verlander, Brian McCann—The Fun Police, Carlos Beltrán, and the rhythmic sound of a trash can being banged on before off-speed pitches thrown by the opposing team. They were the most hated team in the sport and perhaps the most hated team in all of sports. It was quite literally Houston against everybody. The Astros channeled that hate to ninety-five wins in the regular season and the AL West title. They went all the way to the World Series before losing in six games to the Atlanta Braves.

The following year Justin Verlander was back, and so were

the Astros. Houston won an American League–best 106 games in the regular season and waltzed their way back to the World Series by sweeping the Mariners and Yankees. In the Fall Classic, they beat the Philadelphia Phillies in six games.

Vindication. Redemption. The Astros had been dragged through the mud and came out clean on the other side. They were like Andy Dufresne in *The Shawshank Redemption*. Except he didn't crawl through mud. And they weren't innocent.

Either way, Houston proved that they were a great team. They didn't need to cheat to win. They were just that obsessed with winning. Just like Barry Bonds was great and didn't need to take steroids to prove how great he was. But he did anyway, allegedly.

Once they won it all in 2022, I immediately restored the 2017 title and gave everyone their rings back. Everybody except for that rat Mike Fiers. Because here's the thing about the Astros' cheating in 2017. Everyone in the sport was all up in arms because they cheated and got caught. Perhaps if they hadn't cheated, the Yankees would have made it to the World Series. Blah. Blah. Blah.

Well, guess what. The Yankees cheated, too. And so did the Red Sox.

In 2017, the same year the Astros cheated their way to the World Series, the Yankees filed a complaint that the Red Sox had used electronic equipment to steal signs. The league found the Red Sox to be in violation, but also investigated the Yankees and fined them $100,000 after concluding that they, too, had used electronic devices to relay signs to a batter when there was a runner on second base.

Cheaters never win and winners never cheat, right? Bullshit.

22

JOE COOL

JOE BURROW IS A KILLER.

According to my good friend Hal Wingo, when Burrow was nine years old, he played for an AAU basketball team. His team was down eight points with about thirty seconds left and the coach figured that it was over. But it wasn't over. Burrow scored nine straight points, including 7 of 7 from the free throw line, and his team won the game.

His AAU coach was a sociology professor at Ohio University, and after the game he approached Burrow's parents and said that Joe has the kind of qualities you find in first responders, policemen, and serial offenders—that simply put, his blood pressure doesn't change whether he's cutting the lawn or pulling people out of a burning building. The coach explained that he was telling them this because, according to his academic work in criminal sociology, someone who exhibited the same traits as Burrow could have just as easily been the next Dexter—the titular serial killer from the Showtime series. Like I said, he's a killer.

Burrow has made a habit of dicing up defenses everywhere he goes. He won a national title at LSU under Ed Orgeron—Coach O. Before Burrow showed up, Orgeron was just 19–29 as a college head coach. He was more known for his strained vocal range and his two stints as an interim HC (at USC and LSU). In his first year as a starter, Burrow led the Tigers to a 10–3 record and they won the Fiesta Bowl. In year two, they went 15–0 and won the national championship going away. Once Burrow was gone, Coach O went 5–5 and then 6–6 before he was fired. In his career without Burrow, Orgeron was 30–40 as a college head coach. With him he went 28–3 and won a national championship.

The Cincinnati Bengals made Burrow the #1 pick in the 2020 NFL Draft and hoped he would do for them what he did for Coach O and LSU. And boy, did they need him to. For the previous thirty years the Bengals were a punch line. They were completely hapless and an embarrassment to the sport. So much so that people commonly referred to them as the Bungals. Every year they'd be at the bottom of the league and use their first-round pick on someone who would inevitably fail to live up to expectations. We're talking David Klingler, Ki-Jana Carter, Akili Smith, Peter Warrick, David Pollack, and John Ross, to name just a few. At least Carson Palmer and Andy Dalton—the Red Rifle—led the Bengals back to the playoffs, but neither could muster a win in the postseason.

Halfway through Burrow's rookie season with the Bengals, he had completed more passes than anyone else in the history of the league had in their first eight games. But then he tore his

ACL and MCL and was out for the year. The following season, Burrow's first full season in the NFL, he led Cincinnati to a 10–7 mark, won the AFC North, and gave them a home playoff game. He completed 70 percent of his passes, threw for over 4,600 yards and thirty-four touchdowns, and finished second in the league in quarterback rating, trailing only Aaron Rodgers, who was the league MVP.

Once the playoffs started, Burrow was looking for blood. In the wild card round against the Raiders, he threw for 244 yards and two TDs and led the Bengals to their first postseason victory in thirty years.

The thirty years between playoff wins was the longest drought in the league. Think about that. The franchise had gone three decades without winning a playoff game. Three. *Decades.* Burrow won one in his first full season in the NFL. The following week Burrow and the Bengals went on the road to face the #1-seeded Tennessee Titans. The Titans sacked Burrow nine times, tied for the most ever in a playoff game, but Burrow remained unfazed, like Dexter cleaning up a crime scene. He threw for 348 yards and led Cincinnati to its first road playoff victory in the history of the franchise. That's right. First ever. In the history of the franchise. The Bengals had been around for more than fifty years and never won a playoff game on the road. Burrow pulled it off in his first trip to the postseason.

The next week, the Bengals were on the road again, this time at Arrowhead Stadium to take on Patrick Mahomes and the Kansas City Chiefs. The Chiefs led 21–3 late in the second quarter, but Burrow remained calm. He led the Bengals all the way back and took the lead 24–21 late in the fourth quarter. The Chiefs sent the game into overtime with a last-second field goal, but Burrow and the Bengals prevailed, and were on to the Super

Bowl. The eighteen-point deficit they rallied from tied them for the biggest comeback in championship game history. Andy Reid and Patrick Mahomes are one of, if not the best head coach–quarterback duos in the history of the NFL. Burrow went into their house, fell behind by eighteen points, and came back to beat them. Cold-blooded.

Burrow had dragged the downtrodden Bengals all the way to the Super Bowl for what turned out to be another road game. The Bengals played Super Bowl LVI at SoFi Stadium in Los Angeles against the Los Angeles Rams. The Rams not only had home-field advantage; they also had two of the greatest defensive players in the history of the NFL: Aaron Donald and Jalen Ramsey. Burrow had to take them on with a paper-thin offensive line and a rookie as his WR1.

The Rams sacked Burrow seven times, scored a late TD to take the lead, and held off the Bengals by a final score of 23–20.

THE COACH OF THE Rams was Sean McVay. In the NFL, like many professions, it's not what you know, it's who you know, and McVay is a nepo baby. He was born into football. His grandfather coached the New York Giants and then went on to become the GM of the San Francisco 49ers during the height of their success. McVay got his first job in the NFL when he was twenty-two. By the time he was thirty, the Rams had hired him to be their head coach.

McVay was thought to be some sort of offensive prodigy. And boy did he lean into it. He wore sunglasses, put gel in his hair, and demonstrated his youthful energy every chance he got. He looked and felt like the glitz and glamour of Los Angeles.

Now, the Rams had been mediocre before McVay got there,

which is to say that they were coached by Jeff Fisher. He made a habit of going 7–9 or 8–8 just about every year. In 2016 they traded for the #1 pick in the draft and selected Jared Goff. He struggled, like most rookies do in their first year. Fisher was fired after a 4–9 start and McVay took over in the offseason.

In McVay's first season at the helm, the Rams went 11–5 and Goff looked like a totally different quarterback. He'd made a huge leap in his second season in the league, as most highly talented players do, and McVay got all the credit.

The following year Goff led the Rams all the way to the Super Bowl. Again, McVay got all the credit. He was the youngest coach to take a team to the Super Bowl. Their opponent in the big game was, of course, the New England Patriots, coached by Bill Belichick. The biggest storyline in the weeks leading up to the game was the matchup between the young offensive wizard in McVay and the old head defensive mastermind in Belichick.

Although he's nothing more than a mediocre head coach without Tom Brady, Belichick was always an elite defensive coordinator. He had a knack for scheming up ways to take away the opponents' best player. He did it as the defensive coordinator for the Giants. And he occasionally did it with the Patriots. That's why I let him keep half of the rings Brady won for him.

In the end, the Belichick–McVay chess match wasn't much of a matchup. The Patriots won Super Bowl LIII, 13 to 3. The Rams punted on their first eight possessions of the game. Boy wonder was outmatched, outclassed, and embarrassed on the grandest stage.

But it was Jared Goff who got all the blame. In the 2021 offseason, the Rams, at the behest of McVay, traded Goff and a bevy of draft picks to the Lions in exchange for Matthew Stafford.

With Stafford at QB, the Rams wound up as the #4 seed in the NFC, a worse position than when Goff had led them to the #2 and #3 seed in the NFC. But the playoffs fell LA's way because, despite being the #4 seed, they got to host the NFC Championship Game against the #6-seeded San Francisco 49ers.

The Rams trailed by three in the fourth quarter, and Stafford did what Stafford had been known to do—he threw a pass right into the hands of the defense. There wasn't a Rams wideout within five yards of the pass. It looked like Stafford threw it right to 49ers safety Jaquiski Tartt. The ball went right into Tartt's hands . . . and then he dropped it. It was such a sure interception that on the broadcast my friend Joe Buck said, "Stafford airs it out . . . He's picked," before adding, "No, dropped." The Rams would eventually tie the game on that drive and kick a game-winning field goal on their next possession to advance to the Super Bowl against the Bengals.

After the Rams edged out Burrow and the Bengals in the Super Bowl in their own building, the praise was showered upon McVay. It was a fire hose of adulation, but his gelled hair didn't move an inch. The general sentiment was that McVay, the offensive genius, knew that Goff was limited and so the team went out and got Stafford for him and they won it all. His doubts about Goff were validated. The defense, which sacked Burrow seven times and had two generational players leading it, got very little credit.

Do you know what the S in Sean McVay stands for? Sneaky. And I'd had my eye on him for a while. The following season the chickens came home to roost for the Rams. After the team sent out first-round picks like they were Valentine's Day cards in elementary school, the roster was in shambles. The Rams went

5–12 and McVay was ready to jump ship. He started flirting with all sorts of TV networks about becoming a color analyst. The Rams were sinking, and he was not going down with the ship. He was looking for an escape route. Whoever came up with the phrase "When the going gets tough, the tough get going" probably didn't mean the tough get going to the broadcast booth. McVay was a scared chicken, looking to avoid any culpability for the fall of the Rams.

McVay may have this reputation as an offensive genius, but I think his real superpower is avoiding any blame. He was stonewalled in a Super Bowl but put it all on Jared Goff. And Goff turned out to be a really good quarterback under renowned QB whisperer Dan Campbell, by the way. Stafford's pass should have been picked off by Tartt. The Niners should have gone to the Super Bowl. Burrow would have killed them. The chickens came home to roost. McVay is a scared chicken. Throw it all in a pot. Mix it all together with a big ladle. And you know what the end result is? My world-famous ringless soup. Sean McVay: no ring.

In fact, you know who would kill to have that ring? That's right. Joe Burrow. A Super Bowl champion in my personal record book.

23

BETTER NEVER THAN LATE

LET'S TAKE A TRIP BACK TO JANUARY 2003. *FRIENDS* WAS IN its penultimate season, Eminem's "Lose Yourself" was the top song on the charts, and the Fiesta Bowl was for all the Tostitos.

The #1-ranked and defending champion Miami Hurricanes came into the game riding a thirty-four-game win streak. They were coached by Larry Coker, who was fifty-five years old going on seventy-five. He'd coasted to a national championship the year before with Butch Davis's players. I honestly think I could have coached the Canes to the title in '01. A record thirty-eight players from that roster went on to be drafted in the NFL.

Back in 2003 a computer decided who the best teams in college football were and selected the top two to play in the Bowl Championship Series (BCS) National Championship Game. The computer selected the Ohio State Buckeyes, who were coached by a sweater vest named Jim Tressel, to face Miami that night in Tempe, Arizona.

The game was tied at seventeen at the end of regulation, and it was up to college football's funky overtime rules to decide a national champion. Rotating possessions from your opponent's 25-yard line is not how football works, but I digress.

Miami got the ball first and scored a touchdown to put them up 24–17. Ohio State moved the ball to the 5-yard line, but faced a fourth down and 3. The game was on the line. The national championship was on the line. All the Tostitos were on the line.

Buckeyes quarterback Craig Krenzel threw a pass to the front right corner of the end zone intended for Chris Gamble, but it fell incomplete. There was no time on the clock. Actually, there was no time on the clock for the entirety of overtime because of college football's funky overtime rules. Again, not how football works. But the game was over.

The next five seconds felt like a lifetime.

Krenzel fell to his knees and took his helmet off in anguish.

Miami players rushed out onto the field.

Confetti started to fall.

The police began to escort Coker toward midfield to shake hands with the sweater vest.

Miami National Championship shirts were handed out on the sidelines. You know, those really big ones that fit over the shoulder pads. It's a weird look and I'm surprised we haven't found a better way to do it.

Fireworks went off above the stadium.

A few moments later Rick Pitino ejaculated.

Wait. Stop. I got my college sports controversies mixed up there. That happened later in 2003 on a table in an Italian restaurant in Louisville and it took fifteen seconds. Not five. A big difference. Rick, my apologies. I'm just glad there wasn't any garlic bread in the restaurant that night.

Back to those five seconds in Tempe.

In that time, twenty babies were born around the globe.

Hurricanes wide receiver Andre Johnson walked off the field, caught over 1,000 passes for the Texans, and continued on to Canton.

Americans consumed 2,750 hot dogs, 1,750 slices of pizza, and 35,000 Coca-Cola products. We are fat.

Also in those five seconds, the knee of Canes running back Willis McGahee, which was ruptured in the fourth quarter, healed and he rushed for over 1,000 yards and 13 touchdowns in his first season with the Buffalo Bills.

Speaking of the Bills, Miami quarterback Ken Dorsey became their quarterbacks coach, worked his way up to offensive coordinator, and then got fired after the team lost a game to the Broncos because they had twelve men on the field during what would have been a game-ending missed field goal. Obviously, that was the offensive coordinator's fault.

Jeff Bezos made $20,000.

After seeing McGahee's knee buckle, Krenzel wisely pivoted to insurance and became one of the top agents in the Midwest.

Five hundred lightning bolts struck the earth.

Ohio State's freshman running back Maurice Clarett tried to go straight to the NFL but ended up in prison.

Canes tight end Kellen Winslow, Jr., whose TD catch in

overtime made him the MVP of the game, went to the NFL, but he ended up in prison, too.

Roughly 15,800 tons of water flowed over Niagara Falls.

Ohio State's head coach, the sweater vest, wrote a book about responsibility and handling adversity and was then fired for not taking responsibility and mishandling adversity. His lies and withholding of information have tarnished the sweater vest forever. I haven't seen one worn since.

The world record for solving a Rubik's Cube was broken.

Bettors who took the Buckeyes on the money line ripped up their tickets. Those of us who had Miami minus 11.5 had already ripped up ours.

The championship parade from Bayfront Park to the Miami-Dade courthouse on Flagler Street was scheduled.

Greg Cote filed his column for the *Miami Herald.*

As soon as Cote hit send on his column, an official, and not the one closest to the play, threw a penalty flag for pass interference on Miami defensive back Glenn Sharpe.

Get outta here. The Canes won.

Greg Cote, *Miami Herald* columnist and host of *The Greg Cote Show with Greg Cote*

IT WAS THE OFFICIAL BCS NATIONAL CHAMPIONSHIP GAME on that third day of 2003, but to Miami Hurricanes fans and to Stugotz you can drop the C because that will forever be the BS championship game.

The one Terry Porter stole and gave to Ohio State, right? He was the field judge who threw The Flag. It was the flag thrown so late it still hasn't fallen to earth. The notorious

hanky is fluttering somewhere over Tempe twenty-one years later, grinning, still mocking Miami.

By the way, Back in My Day we had no idea what any of the officials' names were and we liked that. Didn't know the buff ref was Ed Hochuli, didn't know the field judge was Terry Porter, and didn't want to. You shouted "Kill the Ump!" never once considering the umpire had a name or for that matter was even a human being.

Back in My Day you called umpires "Blue" and football refs "Zebras" and that was that. Now? For the love of Dean Blandino, now we know all their names and there are even retired refs in the booth as experts because we replay and scrutinize every dubious call nowadays like the FBI dissecting the Zapruder film in 1963.

Where was I?

Oh yeah, so it was a really late flag. Got it. Canes fans after the 31–24 Fiesta Bowl loss to the Buckeyes needed an excuse and got one: a small yellow flag, gift-wrapped.

But two things need to be said in the clarity of two decades' retrospect:

1. Stugotz does not feel this strongly about any game or result unless it involves a number. Clearly he had Miami covering 11½ and still blames Porter for his personal loss, not yet having done the math that would tell him nobody covers 11½ under the college overtime rules of the day.

2. Hey, Miami and its fans: you'd won your fifth national title the season before and won thirty-four games in a row entering that Fiesta Bowl. Getting a

little greedy, were we? Too good to lose? Needed to blame somebody or find a conspiracy theory when you finally did?

Sure, the Canes may have lost because Porter erred. Maybe not, too.

In any case, as Miami safety Sean Taylor said after that game: "Officials make the calls. That wasn't a turning point. We should never have been in that position."

Porter's call has largely been defended following the initial vitriol.

The National Association of Sports Officials said the call was correct. An analysis by the Big XII Conference concluded Miami defender Glenn Sharpe committed four penalties on the play, two each of holding and pass interference. In 2007, *Referee Magazine* called Porter's one of the eighteen best calls in sports history. (What, they couldn't find enough good calls to round it up to twenty? And who knew there was a *Referee Magazine?* Never heard of it or read it, but cancel my subscription anyway.)

Miami had a chance served on a silver platter to survive the controversial call and extend that game into a third OT, but failed on four straight downs to score from first and goal at the Ohio State 2.

Was that Porter's fault, too?

The Hurricanes were pretty good the next few years after that '03 Fiesta Bowl, but then cascaded into twenty years of mediocrity that is still ongoing. It includes a current 1–11 run in Bowl games.

Miami fans ask me all the time, "When will The U be back?"

My stock answer: "When your last two postseason games haven't been losses in the Cheez-It Bowl and then a loss to Rutgers."

If it makes you feel better, Canes fans, just go ahead and blame Terry Porter for the last twenty years.

24

MVPLEASE

THERE ARE WAY TOO MANY FRIVOLOUS DEBATES SURROUNDing the Most Valuable Player Award in almost every sport these days. And that's coming from a guy who's made a living having nothing but frivolous debates.

All too often the writers, pundits, and analysts will overthink their MVP vote with tired questions like: What does valuable really mean? Shouldn't LeBron James be the MVP every year? What if you put Player A on Team Y and vice versa with Player B on Team Z? Should we just vote for the best player on the best team? Enough already. These lazy narratives have cost too many deserving players some well-earned hardware. Hell, Kendrick Perkins went on *First Take* in 2023 and injected race into the NBA MVP conversation. Plenty of voters coincidentally found a way to vote for Joel Embiid instead of Nikola Jokić even though the Joker led the Nuggets to the top seed in the West and went on to win the title. I'm sick and tired of it. Do you want some rules? OK, I'll give you some rules.

Rule number one. You have to be the best player on your own team. It seems obvious, right? The award is presumably given to the best player in the league, so you would think that that player was the best player on his own team. But you would be mistaken. Have you ever heard of Justin Morneau? I didn't think so. He was a first baseman for the Minnesota Twins who barely beat out Derek Jeter for the AL MVP in 2006. And he was the third-best player on his own team, but the writers inexplicably voted him as the best player in the American League. Both Joe Mauer and Johan Santana, guys I've actually heard of, had better seasons than Morneau. Choosing a nobody like Justin Morneau over Derek Jeter is unthinkable, especially when you consider the fact that the Yankees had the best record in baseball that year. Jeets, the MVP is now yours. Congratulations. You won a lot of trophies in your day, but not that one—until today. Now I have to be honest. I thought about taking it away for what you did as the CEO of the Marlins, but I'm going to let you keep it.

You would think that after the Morneau debacle voters would have realized their mistake and made sure not to repeat it, but, again, you would be mistaken. The following season they gave Jimmy Rollins of the Phillies the NL MVP when his double-play partner, Chase Utley, was much better than him. Phillies first baseman Ryan Howard, who won the award the year before, was better than him, too. Matt Holliday of the Rockies should have been the MVP that year and now is, according to this book. He hit .340 with 36 home runs and 137 RBI for a

Rockies team that went to the World Series. Sorry, Jimmy. If it's any consolation, you do edge out WWE superstar Seth Rollins, Rollins College, and former NBA player Tree Rollins in my Rollins hierarchy.

It's embarrassing that I have to do this, but rule number two is just as obvious as rule number one. You can't play for a team that finishes in last place and win the MVP Award. You can't do it. The major league baseball writers screwed this up in 1987 when they gave Andre Dawson of the Cubs the MVP. Sure, he led the league in home runs and runs batted in, but the Cubs finished in last place in the NL East that year. For you younger readers—yes, the Cubs were in the NL East. Weird, right? It gets even weirder. There were six teams in the division. The Cubs finished sixth out of six. That's bad. Dawson had a great season, but he provided zero value to the Cubs. Take him off the team and where do they finish? Sixth. The same spot they finished with him. The Andre Dawson rule is rule number two. Ozzie Smith—The Wizard of Oz—led the Cardinals to first place in the NL East (yes, it's also weird that the Cardinals were in the NL East) and a trip to the World Series. He was your NL MVP in 1987.

Finishing in last place in your division is a no-no. That's obvious to everyone except MLB voters in 1987. It's also obvious that in order to win the MVP Award you have to lead your team to the playoffs. Kareem Abdul-Jabbar was dominant in 1975–76 for the Lakers, but they went 40–42 and missed the playoffs. Three teams ahead of them in their division advanced to the postseason. As great as Kareem was that year (27 points, 17 rebounds, 5 assists, and 4 blocks per game), there's no way he was the Most Valuable Player. His stats were great, but a real MVP would have made his teammates around him better and gotten into the playoffs. Rule number three. You have to make the playoffs. Dave Cowens put up 19 and 16 for a Celtics team that had the best record in the Eastern Conference that season. Big Red, congrats on another MVP.

But making the playoffs is not enough, and I'm not done with rule number three. In order to be eligible for the MVP Award, you need to do more than just sneak your team into the postseason. You need to have home-court/field/ice advantage in the first round. That's not too much to ask, is it? Russell Westbrook averaged a triple-double in 2016–17. Big deal. The Thunder finished in sixth place in the Western Conference. You have to do better than that. James Harden averaged 29 points, 11 assists, and 8 rebounds and led the Rockets to fifty-five wins and the #3 seed in the West. He also shot better from the floor, the free-throw line, and the three-point line than Westbrook. The Beard was your 2017 NBA MVP.

The same goes for Nikola Jokić—The Joker—in 2021–22. Yes, you dragged your team to sixth in the West without Jamal Murray. You had a great season. You earned a spot on First Team All-NBA, but you were not the MVP of the league. Giannis Antetokounmpo was. He led the Bucks to fifty-one wins, which was tied for the second most in the Eastern Conference, and he did it on both ends of the floor, the Greek Freak finishing sixth in Defensive Player of the Year voting.

Listen, I know the MVP is a regular-season award. All voting should take place before the postseason begins. I get all of that. But if the voting is close and one guy absolutely craps the bed in the playoffs, the league should be able to reach out to enough voters to flip the award to the other guy. They should. If the league hasn't announced the award, they should be able to give it to the guy who kept his pants dry in the postseason.

Joel Embiid was named the NBA MVP in 2023 because Kendrick Perkins injected race into the conversation. He beat out Nikola Jokić for the award. Embiid and the Sixers led the Celtics three games to two in the Eastern Conference Semifinals. They had a fourth-quarter lead in Game 6 in their own building, but they collapsed and lost the game. Embiid, the supposed Most Valuable Player, did not get a touch in the last four minutes of the game. He then MVPeed all over himself in the decisive Game 7 in Boston, going 5 for 18 from the field in a blowout loss. The streak down his shorts wasn't the only streak of note that night. His streak of never advancing to the Conference Finals in his career continued. Meanwhile, Jokić and the Nuggets coasted to the NBA title. Rule number four—if the MVP wets the bed in the playoffs, the league has the right to give it to someone else.

The fifth rule for MVPs is simple. If the story of the season can be told without mentioning you, then you weren't the MVP. Narratives matter.

Here's what happened in the NBA in 2005–06.

- The Miami Heat won the first championship in franchise history, beating the Mavericks four games to two in the Finals.
- Dwyane Wade averaged 34.7 points per game in the Finals, the third-highest average all time, and was named Finals MVP.
- Kobe Bryant scored 81 points in a game against the Raptors. It was the second-most points scored in a game in NBA history.
- Commissioner David Stern instituted a dress code.
- LeBron James became the youngest player in NBA history to be named MVP of the All-Star Game.

- LeBron James and Kobe Bryant were each named Player of the Month in their respective conferences twice.
- The New Orleans Hornets played their home games in Oklahoma City due to Hurricane Katrina.
- Ray Allen broke the single-season record for three-pointers made in a season, with 269.
- Kobe Bryant led the league in scoring with 35.4 points per game. It was the highest scoring average since Michael Jordan in 1986–87.

You know who wasn't mentioned at all in that season recap? You know who was never even named Player of the Month? Steve Nash of the Phoenix Suns, whom the voters gave the MVP Award to.

Nash won the MVP the previous season for leading the Suns to sixty-two wins and the top seed in the Western Conference. You could make the case that he didn't deserve to win the MVP that year either, but 2006 was even more ridiculous. The Suns won eight fewer games in 2006. They got objectively worse. But somehow Steve Nash got rewarded for leading a worse team?

There were at least two better candidates for MVP in 2006. LeBron James, at twenty-one years old, averaged 31 points, 7 boards, and almost 7 assists per game. He was named the MVP of the All-Star Game. He led the lowly Cavs to the fourth seed in the East and took the top-seeded Pistons to Game 7 in the East Semis. He earned a spot on first-team All-NBA. And he did it with a supporting cast that was highlighted by Zydrunas Ilgauskas, Larry Hughes, and Flip Murray.

The other MVP candidate who was better than Nash in 2006 was Kobe Bryant. Kobe averaged more than 35 points per game.

No one had done that since Jordan almost twenty years earlier. He carried the Lakers to forty-five wins. Smush Parker was third on the team in scoring. Kobe scored 81 points in a game. OK? Eighty-one. The Lakers made the playoffs, but they were the seventh seed in the West, so Kobe did not meet my criteria for rule number three. That being said, if there is no other obvious MVP, I am willing to bend on rule number three to reward the best player in the sport, and there's no doubt that Kobe was the best player in the NBA in 2006. LeBron checked all my boxes, though, so he is your 2006 MVP.

MVP RULES

1. You have to be the best player on your own team.
2. Your team can't finish in last place. The Andre Dawson rule.
3. You have to make the playoffs and earn home-field/court/ice advantage in the first round.
4. You can't wet the bed in the playoffs. If you do, the commissioner has the right to give the award to someone else.
5. Your performance has to be a part of the narrative of the season.

And now for the kicker. There is one more piece of business regarding MVP Awards that I have to take care of. I'm not going to make it a rule, but I'm going to make a ruling. Something really stupid happened, but I'm going to erase it from the record books once and for all. In the strike-shortened 1982 season, the NFL writers made the biggest blunder in the history of MVP voting. They gave the award to a kicker. I'm serious. People paid to cover the NFL in 1982 actually thought that the Most Valuable Player in the sport that year was a kicker.

Mark Moseley made 20 of 21 field goals for a Washington Redskins team that went 8–1 in the regular season and earned the #1 seed in the NFC. Moseley made two game-winning field goals and was responsible for seventy-six total points in the regular season. A fine season for a kicker, but an MVP he was not.

The Los Angeles Raiders went 8–1 and earned the top seed in the AFC. They were led by running back Marcus Allen, who accumulated nearly 1,100 yards and scored fourteen touchdowns. I was told there would be no math, but if he scored fourteen touchdowns that means he was responsible for eighty-four points, which is eight more than Moseley. But using points scored is a ridiculous metric. How about the fact that Marcus Allen averaged 122 yards from scrimmage for the top seed in the AFC and led the league in touchdowns? Case closed. How was this even a debate? A Hall of Fame running back or a kicker? Who was more valuable? The majority of sportswriters covering the league at that time went with the kicker?

I swear the media can't get out of its own way sometimes. They have a simple task every year and every year they find new ways to screw it up. Their job is to identify the player who was the most valuable for that particular season. That's it.

Andre Dawson, Baseball Hall of Famer and 1987 NL MVP

I WOULD IMAGINE THAT MOST HALL OF FAME BASEBALL players would suggest your conclusion that being on a last-place team should disqualify one from being named an

MVP would be at best arbitrary and capricious, and at worst insulting, degrading, disrespectful, and irresponsible, as becoming an MVP is a rather difficult feat—and for 99 percent of players would be a career-defining achievement. But not me. No, I wouldn't characterize your argument that way at all, and you're probably wondering why.

Well, it's easy to become an MVP. I mean, they give out two of them a year.

It's easy to hit forty-nine home runs, as evidenced by the seventeen times it had been done in 116 years of baseball prior to 1987. But you're a baseball historian, so you obviously have a great perspective on how rare it was at that time in the Major Leagues.

It's easy to drive in 137 runs, as evidenced by the twenty-two times it had been surpassed in the National League in the previous 116 years. But as a baseball historian, you already knew that, too.

It's easy to win a Gold Glove on two bad knees, playing day baseball at Wrigley Field. Since lights didn't come in until the August following my MVP selection, you know that most people considered right field at Wrigley Field during the day to be the hardest right field there was in the game. It still is. But since you're a baseball historian, you already knew that and took it into consideration.

It's easy to be an MVP in a contract year, but back in those days it was almost always a contract year, as you know. It's easy to prove your worth when you sign a blank contract with the Cubs and let them fill in the amount of $500,000 when no one else would even consider giving you a job in a year of ownership collusion. Sure, it was about 25 percent of what a fair contract would have been, but it's easy to be

an MVP when you're not even in the top two hundred of the highest-paid players in the game, and not even in the top ten highest salaries on your own team. Today, it's probably ten years and $300 million. But you know all about collusion and how free agents were told no one wanted them, because you're a baseball historian and you know all about the collusion years and the penalties owners later paid for colluding.

Most people think the best player having the best season should be voted MVP, regardless of team standing. I know Hank Aaron, Willie Mays, and Ted Williams believed that. I know that because I had conversations with all of them. But you're a baseball historian, so you probably had those same conversations.

You made a great argument, and since you're a baseball historian we should all be satisfied with the case you made.

Congratulations.

The Rebuttal to the Rebuttal

Andre, with that rebuttal you have a better case for being the MVP of this book than you did for being the MVP of the National League in 1987.

25

AMERICA'S TEAM

WHY DO PEOPLE STILL REFER TO THE DALLAS COWBOYS AS "America's Team"? Seriously. Did we vote on this? The Cowboys? It doesn't make any sense. They haven't played in the Super Bowl in damn near thirty years. When is the last time the Cowboys were really Super Bowl contenders? You would have to go back to the days of Troy Aikman, Emmitt Smith, and Michael Irvin—The Playmaker—right?

It's been a comedy of errors for the Cowboys in the postseason since they last won the Vince Lombardi Trophy. Remember when Tony Romo mishandled the snap on what would have been a go-ahead field goal against the Seahawks? How about when Dak Prescott slid down after a long run, but couldn't get the team to the line to spike the ball before time ran out against the 49ers? And we are still calling them America's Team? Not in this book we aren't.

In 1978, a guy by the name of Bob Ryan was working for NFL Films. Not the *Boston Globe* columnist. He was busy covering a Red Sox team that, as we've discussed, blew a fourteen-game lead on the New York Yankees and missed out on the postseason because of Bucky Fucking Dent. This other Bob Ryan was putting together the 1978 highlight film for the Dallas Cowboys and wrote a line referring to them as "America's Team." The great John Facenda voiced it and the name stuck.

Back then it made sense. The Cowboys were coming off a stretch in which they had gone to the Super Bowl three times in the previous four seasons. They had Roger Staubach, Tony Dorsett, and Drew Pearson. Tom Landry was still the coach. They were consistently in the mix.

But that was forty-five years ago. Now they are consistently out of it. Calling them America's Team today is like calling Notre Dame America's Team in college football. There was certainly a time when that nickname was accurate, but that time was long ago. Notre Dame hasn't won a national championship since 1988 when Lou Holtz was slobbering around the sidelines. My friend and former Notre Dame offensive lineman Mike Golic, Jr., wasn't even alive back then.

The Cowboys and Notre Dame have found themselves in oddly similar positions lately, too. They're both good, but not great. They handle their business against the bad teams to the point where people start thinking they're actual contenders. But whenever they play a real contender you get scores like Alabama 42, Notre Dame 14 in the BCS title game, or Minnesota 34, Dallas 3 in the divisional round. People want to believe that they have a real chance of winning it all, but then you get Alabama 31,

Notre Dame 14 in the CFP Semis or Green Bay 48, Dallas 32 in the wild card round. Yes, I do enjoy writing down the scores of these losses.

The Cowboys are out. We need a new America's Team. And America's Team has to play American football, because the NFL is head and shoulders above all other sports in popularity.

Call me old-fashioned, but when I think about America, I think about winners. We won the Revolutionary War. We won both of the World Wars. We invented the car, the plane, the computer. We win. That's what we do. We can't go around having a team that hasn't sniffed the Super Bowl in three decades as our team. We can't do it. America's Team needs to win.

When I think about Americans I think about hardworking, gritty, blue-collar individuals who might be a bit overweight but love to relax and watch football on the weekends while throwing back a few frosty beverages. Real Americans are resilient, hard-nosed, and determined. They work tough jobs. They wear hard hats and steel-toed boots. They work hard and they play hard. Real Americans love football. They love beer. And they love nachos, pizza, cheese, hamburgers, hot dogs, and cake. We. Are. Fat.

When I think about how America was built, I think about manufacturing, infrastructure, industry, and labor. America was built on steam and steel. And it was largely built by immigrants.

If it's obvious to me then it must be obvious to you. America's Team is the Pittsburgh Steelers. The Steelers are tied atop the league with the most Super Bowl wins in NFL history (six). They win. Like America wins. Since 1978, when the Cowboys were first given the America's Team moniker, no team in the NFL has more wins than the Pittsburgh Steelers. The Steelers have not had a losing record in twenty years. The Cowboys have had four.

The Steelers are resilient, just like Americans. The organization stays true to what they believe in. They commit. They ride things out. The Steelers have had only three coaches since 1969: Chuck Noll, Bill Cowher, and Mike Tomlin. The Cowboys have had five since the turn of the century, and by the time you read this they'll probably have moved on to their sixth.

The Steeler fan base is filled with real Americans, who work tough, blue-collar jobs. That fan base was named the best in the NFL by ESPN, by the way. And those fans don't jump through tables or put cheese on their heads. They eat lots of cheese and wave yellow towels around like maniacs, but that's different.

The makeup of the Steeler fan base is just more representative of America than the fan base of the Cowboys. Just look at the famous fans of each team throughout the years. For the Cowboys you have Akron's own LeBron James, New York City's own Jay-Z and Denzel Washington, England's own Kate Bosworth, Las Vegas's own Bryce Harper, former New Jersey governor Chris Christie, and, of course, Skip Bayless. For the Steelers you have Michael Keaton, Reggie Jackson—Mr. October, Jeff Goldblum, Seth Meyers, Arnold Palmer, and Stephen A. Smith. I have always chosen and will continue to always choose Stephen A. Smith over Skip Bayless.

Dallas is all glitz and glamour. It's filled with oil money and get-rich-quick schemes. People move there to show off their wealth. Pittsburgh is not splashy. It's all grit and grind. It's filled with steelworkers and hourly wages. People stay there to make a living.

There's something about the Steelers that attracts fans nationwide. Maybe it was their success in the 1970s. Maybe it's their gritty, hardworking spirit. Maybe it's the leadership of head coach Mike Tomlin. Whatever it is, there is an allure to the

Steelers that extends far beyond western Pennsylvania. It's hard to explain why, but there's a Steeler bar in every city in America. I'm not making this up. You can't find an Arizona Cardinals bar in Seattle, but you can find ten where fans of the Steelers congregate on Sundays to suck back Yuenglings and watch the Black and Yellow.

We can't agree on much in America, but we can agree on this. The Cowboys are losers and do not represent America. The Steelers are winners and are now known as America's Team.

Mike Golic, Jr., former Notre Dame offensive lineman who spent a training camp with the Pittsburgh Steelers

FIVE PARAGRAPHS. THAT'S ALL IT TOOK FOR THE NOTRE Dame slander to show up. I'm not mad or disappointed, though . . . because now I get to respond in this chapter and officially call myself an author in my Twitter bio. How 'bout that!

Yes, teams like Notre Dame, the Cowboys, and the Yankees are hardly the prolific championship-winning machines they once were. Yes, the Steelers are a stable franchise with a well-respected head coach who always wins more than he loses, more recent Lombardi trophies in their cabinet, and a fan base whose culture includes putting fries on their sandwiches and freestanding basement toilets (look it up). Seems to be a winning equation.

But even that is starting to feel like a distant memory now. Mike Tomlin was asked about his job status for the first time in my lifetime in 2023, their QB Room has been a mess

going back to the last few seasons with Big Ben, and they haven't made it out of the Wild Card Weekend since 2017.

Now, we *could* quibble over what it actually means to be "America's Team." Maybe an organization all about brand recognition, nostalgia, and a charismatic figurehead is actually the perfect representation for America? BUT, if we want to stick with the premise that this is about what have you won for me lately, there's really only one option. . . .

The Patriots are America's team. Mired in controversy because of a win-at-all-costs attitude, they've been the most dominant force in the history of the league at a time when winning consistently has never been harder. Their Hall of Fame QB Tom Brady is the archetypal NFL underdog story, going from being pick 199 to becoming the most decorated player in the history of the sport, marrying a supermodel, and retiring after getting wasted on a boat in Florida. Their coach spoke softly and carried a big stick, while also dressing for comfort over style, just like the rest of America. They've won all of their Lombardi Trophies since Y2K. Hell, their fans hail from one of the thirteen original colonies, for crying out loud. And maybe most important . . . everyone else hates them! What's more American than that?

Jessica Smetana, host and producer for Meadlowlark Media and *The Dan Le Batard Show with Stugotz,* who grew up as a Steelers fan and graduated from Notre Dame

---

IN THIS CHAPTER, STUGOTZ TAKES THE OLD SPORTS CLICHÉ "Who is America's team?" and turns it into a sociological and anthropological discussion on what it means to be American. It is a topic that if broached by Dan Le Batard on *The Dan Le Batard Show with Stugotz,* Stugotz would surely tune out within fifteen seconds. Stugotz, the Stugotz is strong in you.

Stugotz does have a point, though. If we are defining "*America's team*" based solely on rings, which many of Stugotz's arguments boil down to, then yes, the Dallas Cowboys have underperformed for decades. If we are deciding the Cowboys' status based on America's favorite metric, capital, then it's hard to argue that a brand worth over $9 billion according to *Sportico* does not occupy a prominent position in the American sports psyche. This estimate is the highest of any sports team, not just in America, but in the world.

As a Steelers fan born and raised in Chicago, I can attest to the fact that we are *everywhere.* My grandparents, both Pittsburgh natives, were season ticket holders before the Steelers became a championship-caliber operation. There was no way their granddaughter was going to grow up a fan of any other team. Steelers fandom is inherited. And it travels. When Pittsburghers move away from the city for school, new jobs, or other opportunities, their Terrible Towels travel with them. Stugotz may not know about the significant decline of the steel industry in Pittsburgh since the '80s, and the subsequent rebirth of the city as a tech and healthcare hub, but he's absolutely right that Pittsburgh's obsession with the Steelers is not bound by geography.

All things considered, I'm OK with Stugotz referring to the Steelers as "America's Team," mostly because I think he means it as a compliment.

26

DIVINE ORDERS

DO YOU REMEMBER WHEN LOYOLA (CHICAGO) MADE A CINDER-ella run to the NCAA Men's Final Four in 2016 as a #9 seed? It was awesome, right? That's what March Madness is all about. A plucky underdog who comes out of nowhere, slays a bunch of Goliaths, cuts down the nets at the Regional Final, and heads to the Final Four. That team and that run was unforgettable.

Do you remember who their leading scorer was? Leading rebounder? Anyone on their roster? What about the name of their coach? You can't. Can you? No one can. Hell, you just nodded right along when I said that they made it to the Final Four in 2016 (it was 2018) and how they were a #9 seed (they were an #11 seed). The only thing you actually remember about Loyola (Chicago)'s run was their team chaplain, Sister Jean.

TOP 5 ATHLETES AND ENTERTAINERS WHO CONNOTE A MEMBER OF THE CLERGY

OLI

Brian Cardinal
Twisted Sister
Charlie Chaplin
Bishop Sankey

5. Kendrick Nunn
4. Reggie White, The Minister of Defense
3. Kentavious Caldwell-Pope
2. Deacon Jones
1. Priest Holmes

Who could blame you for remembering only Sister Jean? She was everywhere for the entire month of March and then some. How often do you hear about a ninety-eight-year-old basketball-loving nun affiliated with a team that keeps knocking off teams that are supposedly better than them? The media has a habit of overdoing a story that piques the national interest (e.g., Linsanity). This time they just happened to do it about someone who wore a habit.

The problem was that Sister Jean got allll of the media coverage. Not half of it. Not three-quarters of it. All of it. OK? She was everywhere. Newspapers, *SportsCenter, Good Morning America, First Take,* local news shows, blogs, radio shows, podcasts. You name it. You couldn't go more than three minutes without seeing her face on a TV, computer, newspaper, or phone. Highlight packages from Loyola (Chicago) games showed more cutaways to her in the crowd than they did actual plays from the game. In the minds of the television executives, she was *the* story.

But let's not forget that without the players winning those games they were not supposed to win, the Sister Jean phenomenon does not happen. The players, and to a lesser extent the coaches, did the work to win those games. They made the shots. They grabbed the rebounds. They carried the crosses. They dove for loose balls. They played tough defense. And they deserved the credit. Not some nun who said a prayer before they went out to the layup line. Those players earned the fifteen minutes of fame that being a part of a double-digit seed advancing to the Final Four usually provides. Even when the players or the coach were interviewed—which was rare, by the way—they had to answer questions about Sister Jean. The whole thing was nauseating.

Now, I want it on the record that I think Sister Jean is a lovely person, but there's a little Stugotz in everyone and she ate that attention up for breakfast, lunch, and dinner. Hell, she was still dining out on that run in August 2023, when she threw out the first pitch at Wrigley Field on her 104th birthday.

I bet if you got some of those Loyola (Chicago) players in a confessional they'd tell you that their experience of making it to the Final Four was not all that it should have been because a nun who was supposed to be showing them the light was hogging all of it.

Much to my chagrin, the Ramblers of Loyola (Chicago) out of the Missouri Valley Conference became synonymous with Sister Jean. I am certain that there were plenty of compelling stories about the players on that Loyola (Chicago) roster. I am certain the coach, Porter Moser, had a backstory the casual March Madness fan would have been interested in. But we didn't get those stories. Announcers weren't relaying those anecdotes. All we got was Sister Jean this. And Sister Jean that. They made multiple Sister Jean bobbleheads, for Christ sakes!

If we're being honest, Sister Jean's act wasn't even original. A nun who really likes basketball? May I present you with Whoopi Goldberg. And Whoopi wasn't just some team chaplain. She was the coach of the New York Knicks. *And* she could sing!

Even though Sister Jean didn't play a single second for Loyola (Chicago), she did score a lot of interviews. She definitely assisted in boosting her own ego. She yanked the spotlight away from a group of eighteen- to twenty-two-year-olds who worked hard and earned that attention. And she blocked the American people from hearing about the stories of the players on the court. Sister Jean should have known better. Shame on her. And shame on the media for forcing the Sister Jean story down our throats at every turn throughout that magical run. They should have known better, too.

Here's some divine intervention for you. I'm pretty sure the Bible says an eye for an eye, so for the errors in judgment by a woman of the cloth, I am hereby compelled to take down the cloth hanging in the Joseph J. Gentile Arena in Chicago. By the powers vested in me by the sports gods, I now pronounce that the Loyola (Chicago) Ramblers have never made it to the Final Four. You may now kiss that banner goodbye.

27

SEEN THE LIGHTS GO OUT ON BROADWAY

JOE NAMATH IS A CULTURAL ICON. AND HE WAS A NEW YORK Jet. I could count on one hand the number of New York Jets who were also cultural icons. Now that I think about it, I only need one finger to do the count because it's just Namath. Broadway Joe.

The Jets drafted Namath first overall in the 1965 AFL Draft and he quickly became a media darling. He stood out for his white cleats and the full-length fur coats he wore on the sidelines. He dated celebrities like Janis Joplin and Raquel Welch. He was a pitchman for Ovaltine, Noxzema, and Hanes. He landed acting roles in feature films and numerous television shows during and after his NFL career. He even hosted his own talk show during his fifth season as a professional football player. Namath was the first true celebrity quarterback.

In 1968 Namath led the Jets to the AFL Championship and a spot in Super Bowl III against the Baltimore Colts. To that point the AFL was seen as an inferior league, having lost the first two Super Bowls to the NFL's Green Bay Packers. Three days before the game Namath famously guaranteed that the Jets would win. They beat the Colts 16–7 and Namath was named Super Bowl MVP.

Not only did Namath make good on his guarantee, but he also became the first quarterback to win both a Super Bowl and a national championship in college. Namath played his college ball at Alabama, which, for reasons that remain unclear to me, has an elephant as its mascot, which I suppose is actually fitting, because we need to talk about the elephant in the room.

Joe Namath does not belong in the Pro Football Hall of Fame.

He is a legend; there is no debating that. But he was also legendarily bad at playing quarterback. All the best quarterbacks who have ever done it win a lot more than they lose. Namath's Super Bowl guarantee made people think he was a winner, but a winner he was not. Joe "Willie" Namath lost more games than he won in his career. He went 62–63–4.

It turns out that Broadway Joe couldn't hit the broad side of a barn, either. Namath played for thirteen years. In more than half of them he completed less than 50 percent of his passes. His career completion percentage was 50.1 percent.

In fairness to Namath, he actually completed 56 percent of his passes. It's just that 6 percent of them were caught by the defense. Namath threw a whopping 220 interceptions in his career. That's more than one and a half per game. He led the league in picks on four separate occasions. In 1968, the Jets' Super Bowl season, Namath had a game against the Bills in which he threw five interceptions and three of them were returned for touchdowns.

The best quarterbacks of all time are accurate, throw two times more touchdowns than interceptions, and, again, win a lot more than they lose. Namath did none of those things. He pales in comparison to even the mediocre quarterbacks of the last fifteen years. Take Andy Dalton, for example, The Red Rifle.

	NAMATH	DALTON
WIN-LOSS RECORD	62-63-4	83-78-2
TDS	173	246
INTERCEPTIONS	220	144
COMPLETION PERCENTAGE	50.10%	62.50%
4,000-YARD SEASONS	1	2
20+ INT SEASONS	5	1
SEASONS WITH MORE TDS THAN INTS	2	12

Spare me all this talk about how they played in different eras. Dalton was average at best. He never won a playoff game. His numbers should not shine next to those of a guy who has been heralded as an icon of the sport.

Namath is the most overrated player in the history of the

sport. I could name ten Jets quarterbacks who were better than him. In fact, I guarantee it.

1. Chad Pennington
2. Vinny Testaverde
3. Mark Sanchez—The Sanchize. He took us to back-to-back AFC Championship games.
4. Ken O'Brien
5. Pat Ryan
6. Richard Todd
7. Ryan Fitzpatrick—Fitzmagic
8. Ray Lucas
9. Brett Favre for that one year
10. And Tom Tupa, who was an even better punter than he was a quarterback

I could keep going. Sam Darnold, whom the Jets drafted third overall in 2018, was a bust, but he still managed to complete 60 percent of his passes and throw six more touchdowns than interceptions as a Jet. And he was seeing ghosts out there.

Even Zach Wilson, another bust whom the Jets took in the top five (second overall in 2021), had a year where he completed 60 percent of his throws and had more TDs than picks.

That means I have Namath as the thirteenth-best New York Jet quarterback of all time. Some say that 13 is an unlucky number and maybe they're right, because Broadway Joe's luck is about to run out.

Namath infamously wanted to kiss the great Suzy Kolber on the sidelines in 2003. Well, I got news for you, Joe. You can kiss that gold jacket goodbye. You're no longer in the Pro Football Hall of Fame.

Mike Greenberg, host of ESPN's *Get Up* and a diehard fan of the New York Jets

STUGOTZ, MANY IS THE TIME THAT I HAVE QUESTIONED your intellect, your integrity, and the very existence of your career, but until now I had always felt strongly about your loyalty. But to take sides against the only true legend—not *one* of the only, but the *absolute* only—in the history of our shared favorite franchise is an act bordering on treason. I don't merely want you silenced, I now want you arrested.

My friend Cris Carter—himself a Pro Football Hall of Famer—always tells me that the honor is not reserved just for the best of the best players, but for those without whom the story of pro football itself could not be told. If indeed that is a reasonable criterion, and—spoiler alert—it most certainly is, then not only is Joe Namath deserving of enshrinement, but he in fact should be privy to all the special rights and privileges reserved for only the most important inductees, because that is the company he keeps. There aren't but a handful of more consequential players in the history of the sport than Broadway Joe, regardless of how many finished with prettier statistics.

Were it not for the force of Namath's charisma, stature, and swagger, the Super Bowl—the literal apex of modern American culture—might never have existed. As you are no doubt aware, the first two NFL-AFL Championship Games were embarrassing blowouts, engineered by Vince Lombardi's Green Bay Packers. The upstart AFL was viewed not only as a punching bag, but as a laughingstock. Curt Gowdy, the legendary announcer who called Super Bowl III for NBC, would later say: "Pete Rozelle told me there was anxiety that if there were another lopsided game, they'd have to scrap the game or create a new formula for it." So Namath didn't just guarantee and engineer the greatest upset in football history; he won the most important game ever played.

Imagine a world today without the Super Bowl. Imagine a Stugotz without a Radio Row in which to run roughshod promoting your podcast, your new book, or whatever product it is you will desperately be hawking whenever Dan finally figures out he doesn't actually need you. Imagine the rest of us stuck in the house on a Sunday in February with no football, no wings, and no halftime concert during which you and I are constantly asking our kids: "Do *you* know this song?" That's the world Joe Namath rescued us all from, and as repayment you want to remove him from the Hall of Fame? That would be like a doctor saving your life in the operating room and when you come to you demand his car be towed because it is blocking you in.

Finally, the idea that Namath is anything other than the greatest quarterback in Jets history is not merely blasphemous, it is irretrievably stupid. I watched every snap taken from center by every name on your list and, with all due respect, there's not one of them worthy of blowing dry Namath's fur coat. So, in closing, not only do I vehemently disagree with your take, but I would actually like to make a motion that you be forcibly restrained from ever again calling yourself a fan of the Jets, or from setting foot anywhere on Long Island, until you have issued a heartfelt apology. Do I have a second?

28

MOCK . . . YEAH

THE NFL DRAFT HAS BECOME LOLLAPALOOZA. THEY'RE BOTH multiday events that draw hundreds of thousands of people. At Lollapalooza the fans get to enjoy hours and hours of music from some of the biggest musical acts in the world. At the NFL Draft the fans get to hear 260 or so names read aloud.

The popularity of the NFL Draft is hard to believe. They used to do the whole thing on a Saturday from Radio City Music Hall in New York City. It is now a three-day event that different cities around the country get the privilege to host. Round one is in prime time on Thursday night. Rounds two and three are in prime time on Friday night. And then rounds four through seven are all day on Saturday. Hundreds of thousands show up and millions upon millions watch on television.

The draft is literally an enormous meeting that could be an email. In fact, it used to be. Well, not an email, but a fax. And, in case you forgot, a fax is like an email, except the message shows up on a piece of paper.

The NFL Draft went from being a fax to a rock concert largely on the shoulders of one man: Mel Kiper, Jr.

Mel has become almost synonymous with the draft, and rightfully so. He came out of the womb with that helmet of hair on his head, an eye for NFL talent, and his Big Board. When he was in high school, he hand-delivered scouting reports to Ernie Accorsi, who was then the GM of the Baltimore Colts. Accorsi wisely told him to sell his information to the public, which Mel started doing while he was still in college in 1981.

Back when Kiper first started scouting players, there was no internet. There was no NFL Scouting Combine. Kiper had to do all the grunt work himself. He spent hours on the phone with college coaches around the country just to get basic stats.

In 1980, NFL commissioner Pete Rozelle agreed to allow ESPN to televise the draft for the first time. He was skeptical that it would be a draw for fans, but he was wrong. And Kiper was right.

Mel bet big on the NFL Draft. He thought there would be massive interest in it and he devoted his life to covering it. With the advice from Accorsi, he started an industry where there wasn't one before. The success of his scouting business landed him a job with ESPN providing analysis for its draft coverage in 1984. Kiper was just twenty-three years old.

Mel was a natural on television, giving his unvarnished

thoughts on players. His strident opinions ruffled some feathers along the way, which included, perhaps most famously, Colts GM Bill Tobin for not drafting Trent Dilfer in 1994. Mel could have these takes because he put in the work. He dedicated countless hours every year to grinding the tape so that he could tell you about the footwork of the left guard from McNeese State and the hang time of the punter from Iowa. The guy was and still is like a machine. And that machine runs on pumpkin pie. He eats a piece every single day, which is kind of disgusting to be honest.

It's not just the NFL Draft that's become a behemoth. It's the entirety of NFL Draft season. In my early days in radio, we had two seasons. There was the NFL season and there was waiting for the NFL season. Now, in addition to the NFL season and waiting for the NFL season, we have NFL Draft season. NFL Draft season, which extends from December to May, includes the NFL Scouting Combine every February in Indianapolis, where the league descends to poke, prod, measure, and test players hoping to be selected. It's a little strange if you ask me, but it's content. And they televise it. They put pro days on TV, too. Those are just workouts hosted by individual high-profile colleges to give their draft-eligible players another chance to impress NFL scouts and GMs.

Mel Kiper, Jr., is known as the "father of NFL draft gurus," which isn't exactly a catchy nickname, but it's an accurate one. His work covering the draft spawned an entire industry and a legion of copycats coming for his throne. There is no Todd McShay, Daniel Jeremiah, or any of the other hundreds of NFL Draft analysts out there without him. Mel birthed them all, so he, in many ways, is their father. Honestly, the number of mock drafts available to me nowadays is ridiculous. I can now read multiple mock drafts per day throughout the year. And I do. I love them, and I have Mel to thank for the entire industry.

I've been known to borrow a few takes from the ESPN Radio morning show during my time as a radio host both before, during, and after my own time at ESPN. So, it should surprise no one that I'm going to borrow a take from my friend and ESPN executive Seth Markman. In 2023 Markman told Front Office Sports, "There is no NFL Draft on TV without Mel Kiper. He's an institution. I think he should be in the Pro Football Hall of Fame for what he's accomplished and what he's brought to this TV event."

I co-sign, co-opt, and now co-own that take. And because the gold jacket committee in Canton has been dragging its feet for years, I'll do it myself. Not only does Mel Kiper, Jr., get a gold jacket, he also gets a bust at the Pro Football Hall of Fame for his contributions to the game. Before he showed up the draft was a fax. Now it's a rock concert. And he's Pumpkin Pie Bono.

Mike Golic, nine-year NFL veteran and co-host of *GoJo and Golic* on the DraftKings Network

---

I CAN'T BELIEVE I'M SAYING THIS, BUT STUGOTZ IS NOT as dumb as he looks. First of all, he was obviously smart enough to steal a whole bunch of my takes over the years and use them on his show, and I'm glad he's finally admitted it. He's definitely a weasel. But he's a smart weasel, or, at least, smart at being a weasel. Second, I wholeheartedly agree with him saying that Mel Kiper, Jr., is a rock star. No question.

Mel's work on the draft over the years has been amazing. Unlike Stugotz, Mel actually puts in the work. He watches tape. He talks to scouts. And his opinions are rock solid and based in something concrete.

The NFL Draft is the lifeblood of the NFL in much the same way that recruiting is the lifeblood of college football. Mel realized this early on and made an amazing career for himself in that space. The Pro Football Hall of Fame should absolutely honor Mel for the work he's done in helping to popularize the draft. Quite frankly, they are long overdue in acknowledging how impactful he's been.

But in classic Stugotz fashion, he took what was a great point and went too far with it. The Hall should unquestionably honor Mel, but that doesn't mean that he should get a bust and a gold jacket. The Pro Football Hall of Fame has a mechanism in place to honor commentators like Mel. It's called the Pete Rozelle Radio-Television Award and it's given out annually to a member of the media "for longtime exceptional contributions to radio and television in professional football." Past recipients include John Facenda, Al Michaels, Chris Berman, Tom Jackson, Don Criqui, and Andrea Kremer. How Mel has not already been given this award is beyond me.

The busts and gold jackets are for the players, the coaches, and the executives who have transcended the wonderful game of professional football. I love Mel Kiper, Jr. I have known him for decades and think the world of him, but as good as his analysis is, he's never made a pick. He's never called a general manager and tried to negotiate a trade. He's never had to cut a player. He's never had to listen to the opinions of an owner and factor that in before making his

Big Board. He's never had to consult with the coaching staff and identify specific traits that they want from different position groups. Mel has never had his hand in the metaphorical dirt of running an NFL front office.

Mel's opinions are those of an outsider. He is not the man in the arena. I think Mel would even agree with this.

Does Mel deserve the Pete Rozelle Award for his contributions to the NFL? No question. But a gold jacket and a bust? That's a bit much for me.

29

MR. JONES AND ME

DEFENSE WINS CHAMPIONSHIPS. EVERYONE KNOWS THAT. IT doesn't matter if you're playing football, basketball, baseball, hockey, tennis, or water polo. The better your defense is the better your chances are to win a ring.

We don't talk enough about defense, though. It accounts for half of the games we love, but it doesn't get anywhere near half of our attention. Offense dominates the headlines because scoring points, runs, or goals is flashy. A great offense is exciting. It's easy to see. Preventing points, runs, or goals is boring. A great defense is dull. Oftentimes, it's hard to watch.

The most important defensive positions in baseball are up the middle. Catcher, shortstop, second base, and center field.

Everyone knows that, too. If you want to win the World Series, you better be rock solid at those four positions defensively.

So, to recap. Defense wins championships. Defense is half of the game. In baseball, the most important defensive positions are up the middle.

Hell, Joe Mauer got into the Hall of Fame on the first ballot in 2024 simply because he played catcher. No one even argued that he was a great defensive catcher. He wasn't, by the way. Just the fact that he played catcher was enough.

Now, I'm not sure if Mauer is even a Hall of Famer. He may be in the Hall of Very Good for me. He certainly was not worthy of being a first-ballot Hall of Famer. I mean, Plácido Polanco has more hits than Joe Mauer. So does Jason Kendall. So does Juan Pierre—JP. So does B. J. Surhoff. Barry Bonds had more home runs from 2000 to 2002 than Mauer had in his entire fifteen-year career. Jim Fregosi had more career home runs than Mauer. So did Sixto Lezcano and Ruppert Jones. José Reyes had both more hits and homers than Mauer.

Mauer had only one twenty-homer season. He never drove in a hundred runs. But he got into the Hall of Fame because he was a catcher.

So if an above-average catcher like Mauer got in on the first ballot, then surely the best defensive center fielder of all time would too, right?

Nope. The same rules don't apply for Andruw Jones, apparently. He's been on the ballot since 2018 and he's still not in.

No one, and I mean no one, not even the great Willie Mays, patrolled center field like Andruw Jones did when he was with the Braves. He was a defensive cheat code. He played the position so much shallower than anyone else I've ever seen because he had the reaction time, speed, quickness, and a stride that looked effortless, to get to anything that was hit over his head.

Jones won the Gold Glove at center field in ten straight seasons from 1998 to 2007. Only sixteen other players in the history of baseball have won ten or more Gold Gloves, and all of them are in the Hall of Fame except for Keith Hernandez, Omar Vizquel, and Nolan Arenado, who's still active.

It's rare that the sabermetric nerds and I agree. In fact, when we do, I feel gross. I have to take a shower immediately and cleanse both my body and my soul from the mere proximity to an advanced metric. Take a deep breath. It's about to get unpleasant in here. Andruw Jones is ahead of Willie Mays when it comes to career defensive WAR. He's ahead of Ken Griffey, Jr. In fact, he's ahead of every other outfielder who has ever played the game.

That hurt me to type. I have to go take a cold shower. WAR is hard to wash off. I'll be right back.

Here's the thing about Jones's Hall of Fame case. It's not like he was some slouch at the plate, either. He debuted in the big leagues in August 1996. Just two months later, at nineteen years old, he hit two home runs in his first two at bats in Game 1 of the World Series against the Yankees. He became the youngest player to hit a home run in the Fall Classic, breaking a record previously held by Joe DiMaggio—The Yankee Clipper. Joe Mauer never hit a postseason home run in his entire career. He never won a playoff game, either.

Andruw Jones was named to the All-Star Team five times. In 2005 he led the National League with 51 home runs. He also led the National League with 128 runs batted in. He won a Silver Slugger and finished second in the MVP voting to Albert Pujols—The Machine.

Jones finished his career with 434 career home runs, which

puts him in the top fifty all time. He is one of only four players in the history of baseball to hit four hundred or more home runs and win ten or more Gold Glove Awards. The others to do it were Willie Mays—The Say Hey Kid, Ken Griffey, Jr.—The Kid, and Mike Schmidt.

With a résumé like that, you may be wondering why Jones hasn't already been inducted into Cooperstown. The only knock on him is that his performance fell off a cliff once he turned thirty. That's not a knock to me. Who cares what happened after he turned thirty? From 1998 to 2007 he was the third-most impactful player in the entire sport. The only players with a higher Total WAR in that stretch were Barry Bonds and Alex Rodriguez. And they were juicing. Allegedly.

Speaking of juice, I need another shower and juice cleanse after citing WAR again.

So Andruw Jones didn't age gracefully. Covering that much ground defensively north of thirty would have been impossible. Guess who else didn't age gracefully? Joe Mauer. In Mauer's last five seasons he caught only one game! He was a defensive liability, so they moved him to first base, where he was an offensive liability because he never hit more than eleven home runs in a season.

To me, Jones's Hall of Fame case is unassailable. Offensively, he's a top fifty slugger in the history of the sport. Defensively, he's the best outfielder of all time. This is a no-brainer, especially when you compare him with Mauer. Jones hit nearly two hundred more home runs and drove in over three hundred more runs. Plus, he was light-years ahead of Mauer defensively.

Andruw, listen to me. Get on a bird and go to the middle of nowhere in Upstate New York. It's induction time, because you're a Hall of Famer in my personal record book.

30

TUCK OFF

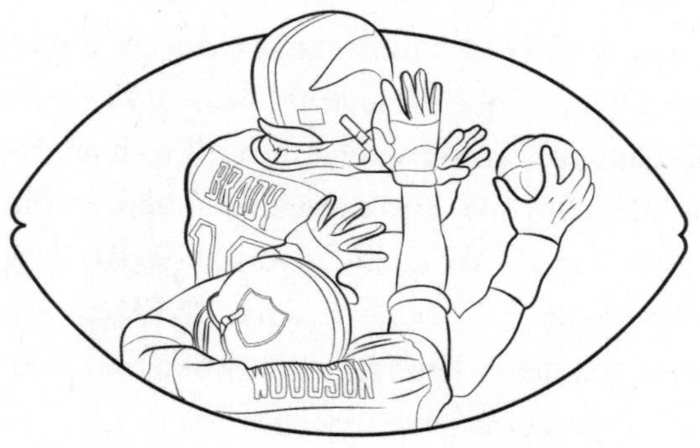

HAVE YOU EVER HEARD OF THE BUTTERFLY EFFECT? NOT THE 2004 movie with Ashton Kutcher, which was terrible. The idea that tiny, seemingly insignificant changes like the single flap of a butterfly's wings in Brazil can lead to massive outcomes like a tornado in Texas. Well, let me tell you about a butterfly named Walt Coleman.

Tom Brady has thrown for the most passing yards in NFL history. He has thrown the most touchdown passes, too. Oh, and he's the only player in the history of the league to win the Super Bowl ten times. He dragged Bill Belichick to six Super Bowls with the New England Patriots and rightfully pocketed half of the rings that customarily go to the head coach. Then he brought the Tampa Bay Buccaneers to the promised land when he was forty-three years old. He's the greatest player to ever put on an NFL uniform. And without Walt Coleman, none of it ever would have happened.

It was a snowy night in Foxboro, Massachusetts, on January 19, 2002. The wind was swirling. Snow was everywhere. You could hardly see more than five feet in front of your face. The Patriots were hosting the Oakland Raiders in the AFC Divisional Round. It was Tom Brady's first-ever playoff game. The Raiders led 13–10 with under two minutes to play, but Brady and the Patriots were driving. On a first and 10 from . . . let's say the Raiders' 42-yard line, because it was hard to tell with all the snow on the ground. Maybe it was the 43-yard line. Maybe it was the 41. Everyone was just guessing, really. And, honestly, it wasn't too different from what happens in a typical NFL game where we have referees guessing where the ball is when the knee, or elbow, or shin, or tuchus of the guy carrying it first touches the ground. And then if there's any doubt about where the referee marked the ball carrier down, we have sixty-year-olds run onto the field with a chain to measure it. The NFL made almost $15 billion in 2022.

But back to that snowy New England night in 2002. On a first and 10 from the Raiders' 42-yard line, Brady dropped back and scanned for an open receiver. He motioned to throw the ball to J. R. Redmond in the left flat but thought better of it and started to bring the ball back to his side. At that moment a blitzing Charles Woodson hit Brady squarely in the right shoulder, knocking him and the ball to the ground. The ball landed in front of Brady and was recovered by the Raiders.

The game should have been over. A couple of kneel-downs by Rich Gannon and the Raiders would have been on to the AFC Championship Game. Drew Bledsoe would have assumed his role as the Patriots' starting quarterback the following season and Tom Brady would have been relegated to the bench. No Super Bowls. No MVPs. No Patriots dynasty. No Deflategate. No TB12 method. No children with actresses and models. Honestly, that sounds like a world I want to live in. But Walt Coleman decided to flap his wings.

Walt Coleman was the referee on that snowy night in the outskirts of Boston. He reviewed the play, which had been ruled a fumble on the field, and determined that there was incontrovertible video evidence to overturn it. He reversed the call and said that it was an incomplete forward pass, and the Patriots resumed possession. A couple of Adam Vinatieri kicks in the snow and both the Patriots dynasty and The Legend of Tom Brady were born.

That play has been ruled a fumble for my entire life. It was as clear as day. Brady was not attempting to throw the ball when Woodson hit him. Calling that an incomplete pass was asinine. Tuck rule, schmuck rule. There's a reason the NFL did away with that dumb rule years later. Because it was garbage.

This one hurts me deeply to say, because Tom Brady has been a guest on my podcast, *STUpodity,* but he fumbled that football and the Raiders clearly recovered it. As far as this record book is concerned, the Raiders won that game. Oakland then beat the Steelers in the AFC Championship Game and dispatched the Rams to win Super Bowl XXVI.

How about that? Another ring for Jerry Rice. Another ring for Charles Woodson. A much-deserved ring for Tim Brown. Jon Gruden gets another ring. Wait. No he doesn't. Gruden proved himself to be racist, homophobic, and misogynistic. His ring goes to Brady and *STUpodity* remains the home for Super Bowl champs.

Randy Scott, *SportsCenter* anchor and diehard Raiders fan

STUGOTZ IS RIGHT? STUGOTZ IS RIGHT. DEFINITIVELY SO. Unassailably so. His logic and arguments are so airtight, even Pat the Patriot couldn't direct someone to take them to a field-level bathroom and deflate them.

Allegedly.

Tom Brady fumbled in the snow and the Patriots dynasty was built on the strength of a rule so bad the NFL repealed it twelve years later.

Walt Coleman. Pshhh. More like Walt Stoleman. More like It'sYourFault Coleman.

As Apple TV+'s *The Dynasty* shows us, Tom Brady may have won over Bill Belichick, but owner Robert Kraft and a group of vocal and senior veterans in the locker room weren't convinced. And we're supposed to believe that if Brady and the Patriots don't get bailed out in the snow by Coleman, if Drew Bledsoe didn't bail them out against Pittsburgh a week later when Brady got hurt, and if the refs hadn't bailed them out in the Super Bowl by not calling PI a dozen times and just running the last four seconds of the game off the clock after Adam Vinatieri's kick had long since fallen down the net . . .

We're supposed to believe that a coach (Belichick) who'd gone 5–11 the previous two seasons and alienated the nine-figure-contract franchise QB (Bledsoe) and ticked off his owner (Kraft) who was building a new stadium on the strength of the popularity and marketability OF that rocket-armed quarterback . . .

We're supposed to believe the quarterback that coach chose (Brady), the one with fewer passing yards per game than Tim Couch and Chris Weinke, and a worse INT percentage than Tony Banks and Jim Miller, we're supposed to believe THAT coach-QB pairing keeps their jobs?

Tuck Rule? More like Tuck Fool, am I right? Because that's what you'd have to be to believe it.

This guy, he gets it. He doesn't want to, but he does.

Field Yates, ESPN NFL Insider and former intern with the New England Patriots

STU, THIS HURTS TO WRITE, GIVEN THAT WE ARE BEST friends.

But I want to get this straight: you're crying over spilled milk in the form of a rule that was properly applied?

Just wanted to make sure we cleared that up.

When an offensive player fumbles through the end zone, it is ruled a turnover and a touchback.

Is it annoying? Sure.

Is it properly applied? Also, yes.

But let's take this one step further: your premise that the Patriots would have handed the keys back to Drew Bledsoe the following season took literally weeks to disprove in real life!

Tom Brady was injured in the AFC Championship Game, launching Bledsoe back into action, as he played a pivotal role in the team's upsetting the heavily favored Steelers on the road.

It was the perfect setup: the crowned prince of the franchise had his moment of clutch and there was another game to play—just seven days later (the Super Bowl is normally fourteen days after the championship game round, but was not in this season).

So, presented with the opportunity to go back to Bledsoe, the widely beloved signal-caller who had recently signed a $103 million contract (then, by far, the largest contract in franchise history), Belichick instead tabbed Brady, playing with a gimpy ankle.

As we all know, Brady would architect a signature game-winning drive that started the legend of who would become the greatest player in NFL history.

Important, but not the only part: in that same game, the Belichick-led defense held the record-setting Rams offense to just two touchdowns (and scored one of their own on a pick-six by Ty Law).

This dynasty was the furthest thing from luck. It was a multipronged (with Brady and Belichick as the primary characters), meticulous, sustained run of dominance.

So take your take and tuck it up your rear.

31

THE TRUTH ABOUT RUTH

IN THE WINTER OF 2022, ESPN RANKED THE TOP HUNDRED baseball players of all time. I love a good list, but I also hate a bad one. And I hated this one. Here's how their top fifteen looked:

15. Mike Trout
14. Greg Maddux
13. Ken Griffey, Jr.
12. Honus Wagner
11. Pedro Martinez
10. Stan Musial
9. Walter Johnson
8. Barry Bonds
7. Mickey Mantle

6. Lou Gehrig
5. Ted Williams
4. Ty Cobb
3. Hank Aaron
2. Willie Mays
1. Babe Ruth

Now, for starters, putting Mike Trout fifteenth is preposterous. The next playoff game he wins will be his first. That wasn't even the most egregious part of the list, though. Look no further than the top, which is actually the bottom. Confusing. I know. Babe Ruth? The best baseball player of all time? I know the sport of baseball skews old because it's full of curmudgeons who are set in their ways, but this has gone too far.

Ruth last played a game in 1935, and he's the best you got? No one who's played the game in the last *ninety years* is better than a fat guy who hit a bunch of home runs off of white guys who were plumbers and electricians in the offseason? Babe Ruth? I don't even have Babe Ruth in my list of the Top 5 New York Yankees of all time.

I will acknowledge that Babe Ruth dominated his era. OK? But the era in which he played (1914–35) was not exactly overflowing with talent. Ruth was playing against guys who were moonlighting as bartenders, vaudeville performers, and tire factory workers. The dedication to the sport was not nearly what it is today. Any professional baseball player of today would dominate Ruth's era. Imagine if you put the aforementioned Trout on the Yankees in 1919. He would obliterate those tomato cans that Ruth was playing against. There's no doubt in my mind that he'd be a bigger sensation than Ruth ever was, but he'd still have no playoff wins.

Ruth was listed as 6-foot-2 and 215 pounds. He was fat and out of shape for his era. Mike Trout is 6-foot-2 and 235 pounds of pure muscle. How many home runs do you think Trout would hit off the 5-foot-7, 135-pound guys who were lobbing the ball over the plate to Ruth? Eight hundred? A thousand? There's no doubt that it is harder to hit a home run off a batting practice pitch in 2023 than it was to hit a home run in 1923 off a live pitcher.

Not only did the competition Ruth played against stink, but there were only sixteen teams. That's half of what the league is today. And back then there was no interleague play. So Ruth played against the same seven teams every season and saw the same pitchers—who, again, were butchers, bakers, and candlestick makers in the offseason—time and time again. I think on principle alone I have to dock Ruth at least half of his World Series rings. In other record books he gets credit for seven, even though in the first series, all he did was go 0–1 with a groundout. I'll give him three, and he should thank me for not taking them all away.

So the competition stunk, Ruth faced the same twenty pitchers over and over again, and those twenty pitchers from the other seven teams in the American League were all small, scrawny, and white. Baseball in 2024 is a global game. There are players from twenty-five different countries today. There is no way that the Babe was facing the best that the world had to offer when he was in the big leagues, because he wasn't even facing the best that the United States had to offer. Baseball in the day and age of Ruth was not integrated. He played against zero Black players, zero Latino players, and zero Asian players. And ESPN has the audacity to call him the greatest baseball player of all time? Please.

Go ahead and plop Babe Ruth from 1923 into today's game. Good luck making contact with a 104-mile-per-hour heater off of Jhoan Duran. Kodai Senga's "ghost" forkball would make the Great Bambino look more like Bambi in headlights. Seriously, he'd have a better chance if he closed his eyes. A slider from Spencer Strider might put him on his feet. The degree of difficulty in today's game is so much higher. Middle relievers practically all throw 95-plus mph. What's the fastest pitch Ruth saw a hundred years ago—75 miles per hour, 80 maybe?

Ranking a guy who wouldn't hit above the Mendoza Line if he were dropped into the present as the best player of all time is terrible. It's a bad job by ESPN. Babe Ruth doesn't belong anywhere near the top of the list. He should be ranked no higher than 50. I have the following six Yankees ahead of him.

Derek Jeter—The Captain. The epitome of leadership. A five-time champion, including the World Series MVP in '00. He was a fourteen-time All-Star. (Ruth was named an All-Star only twice!) Jeets also won five Gold Gloves at one of the most challenging positions on the diamond.

Mariano Rivera—The Sandman. Another five-time champion, including winning World Series MVP honors in '99. Mo is the best closer of all time. Bar none. And he did it when it counted. He has the best postseason ERA of all time (0.70) and the most postseason saves (42). Babe Ruth wouldn't be able to put Mo's cutter in play.

Joe DiMaggio—The Yankee Clipper. Joltin' Joe won nine World Series, racked up three MVPs, and bagged Marilyn Monroe, and his fifty-six-game hitting streak is one of the most unbreakable records in all of sports. DiMaggio had more three-homer games (three) than he did three-strikeout games (one). In fact, he had more home runs than strikeouts in seven different seasons. Plus, like Jeter, he was a stalwart defensively at one of if not *the* most difficult positions: center field. Joe D was a legend. He also gets bonus points for being adamant in his post-playing days that he get introduced as the "Greatest Living Ballplayer," so much so that he once punched Billy Crystal in the stomach for not doing so.

Mickey Mantle—The Mick. Mantle won seven titles, all with the Yankees, and was a twenty-time All-Star. He won three MVP Awards, hit for the Triple Crown in 1956, and won a Gold Glove as a center fielder.

Perhaps you think it's unfair to hold Ruth's circumstances against him, but he wasn't even the best Yankee of his era. The best Yankee of that time was Lou Gehrig—The Iron Horse—a teammate of Ruth's and a much better player. He won the Triple Crown in 1934, two MVPs, and six World Series with the Yankees. Gehrig drove in more runs and hit for a better average than Ruth. He also showed up to play every day. Gehrig played in 2,130 consecutive games, a record that stood for nearly sixty years.

Yogi Berra. Yogi won a record ten World Series with the Yankees. He won three MVPs and was an eighteen-time All-Star. Like everyone else I have ahead of Ruth, Yogi was a lot more impactful defensively as a catcher than Ruth ever was loafing around left field. Plus, Yogi is perhaps the most quotable player in the history of sports. That's not nothing. Coining phrases like "It ain't over till it's over" and "It's like déjà vu all over again" is more impressive than Ruth's entire career.

Lastly, for all of you irate New York Yankees fans who wait for hours on hold just to ask a question to a host on WFAN. First and foremost, thank you. Your rabid fanhood has served me well as a career gasbag. But I would ask all of you this. You hate the

Red Sox, right? You do. Got it. I heard you. No need to scream into the book. So should you even consider someone to be a Top 5 Yankee if they played six seasons for the Red Sox?

Honestly, Ruth isn't even in my Top 5 Players Who Played for Both the Red Sox and the Yankees. He's behind Roger Clemens—The Rocket, Rickey Henderson, Wade Boggs, Don Baylor, Johnny Damon, Alex Verdugo, David Cone, David Wells, and Andrew Benintendi.

32

ZEN AND THE ART OF SUPERSTAR RELIANCE

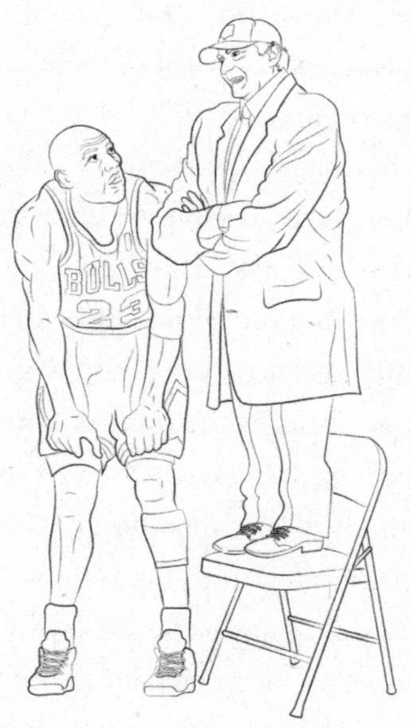

THE FACT THAT ANYONE CONSIDERS PHIL JACKSON THE GREATest NBA coach of all time is laughable. It is laughable, I tell you. Phil Jackson coached Michael Jordan, Scottie Pippen, Horace Grant, and then Dennis Rodman. Eight titles later he goes to LA and coaches Kobe Bryant and Shaquille O'Neal and racks up five more. The winning was not following him. I can assure you of that. He was following the winning.

Let's start with Chicago. Jordan was such a superhuman competitor and athlete that someone was going to coach him to a handful of titles. I mean, he's the greatest basketball player we've ever seen. Period. End of discussion. Doug Collins would have won eight. Phil ended up winning eight. I would have won eight. You would have won eight. We all would have won eight. In fact, it might be the single thing all of humanity—rich, poor, Black, white, male, female, and on and on—has in common. We all share the common trait of having eight rings if we had coached that team. And if Bulls GM Jerry Krause hadn't run Phil, Scottie, and everyone else out of town after the '98 season, we all would have won nine or ten.

Quickly on Krause, who once said, "Players and coaches don't win championships; organizations win championships." Listen. You would not have won a single championship without Michael Jordan. OK? Not one. They put you into the Basketball Hall of Fame in 2017 and now I'm taking you out. Players don't win championships? That is the most absurd thing said in this entire book and I didn't even say it.

Not only did the Bulls organization have nothing to do with the eight-peat, but Phil had nothing to do with it, either. I don't want to hear about the triangle offense, which was all Tex Winter, by the way. It doesn't matter what offense you run. It matters who's running it. And Michael was running it. You could run the square, the circle, the rectangle offense. I don't care what offense. Whatever shape you want to put in, Michael was going to run it, execute it, and win you titles. I don't care.

Triangle offense. Phil Jackson. Some deep thinker. Get the hell out of here. He was a stoner from the '60s and '70s. Which is fine, but that's who he is. I don't want to hear about it. He's a hippie. And the fact that he's this ethereal guy. He's doing yoga, meditation, this and that, he's got all the answers. Give me a break. What he had was Michael Jordan. That's what he had. And then he had Kobe and Shaq.

He had nothing to do with the winning in Chicago, but he was close to it. And just by his being in the same vicinity as Michael Jordan led people to believe that he was this great coach. Sound familiar *ahem Belichick* *ahem Brady*? Sorry, something in my throat. But Dr. Jerry Buss believed it and brought Phil out to coach the Lakers. LA had the best player in the sport in Shaq and a guy in Kobe who was doing his best MJ impersonation. Bing, bang, boom. They win three titles. Imagine that!

Shaq gets traded to Miami, where he wins a title alongside Dwyane Wade, and suddenly the great Phil Jackson can't win anymore. Imagine that! He cranks up the excuse machine, walks away from the Lakers, and writes a book about how he can't coach Kobe. He comes back the next year and the Lakers don't win a damn thing until they trade for Pau Gasol, one of the best big men in the world. With Kobe and Pau the Lakers win two more championships. Imagine that!

So Phil won eight with Michael, three with Kobe and Shaq, and then two more with Kobe and Pau. If I'm doing my math correctly, that means he's never won a title without having a top-two or -three player in the league. Really the best player in the league. Never. He's never done anything.

And then he goes to the Knicks and steals James Dolan's money, which I don't mind, by the way. But he doesn't have the guts to coach there because the team wasn't any good. And he doesn't want to expose himself. Who was in charge of getting the players for that team? That's right. Phil Jackson. So I don't want to hear about Phil.

And I don't want to hear about Steve Kerr, either. Kerr, who played for Phil Jackson with the Bulls, didn't have the chutzpah to work for Phil and coach the Knicks in 2014. Instead he goes to Golden State and starts winning with Mark Jackson's players.

Steph Curry is an all-time great point guard. He learned at the hip of another all-time great point guard in Mark Jackson. It's not Mark Jackson's fault that the fruits of his tutelage did not fully blossom until the 2014–15 season. Jackson got canned and Steve Kerr stepped in and got all the credit.

Steph Curry and Klay Thompson are two of the greatest shooters in the history of basketball. Draymond Green was a defensive wizard. They were inevitably going to win championships. The league was changing, and Mark Jackson was the catalyst. Not Steve Kerr. Steve Kerr may have been the coach for four championships, but he was drafting off the work that Mark Jackson did.

Do you want to know how I know that Steve Kerr is not a genius head coach? At the start of training camp prior to the 2015–16 season, he took a leave of absence to rehabilitate his ailing back. I would have thought that Steph needed the break to heal his back after carrying Kerr to the title a few months earlier, but what do I know. So Kerr was out of the picture and the Warriors named Luke Walton, the son of the late great Bill Walton, as the interim head coach. Walton had never coached an NBA game in his life.

The Warriors started the season 24–0. Under Walton's guidance they went 39–4, the second-best start in league history. But I'm supposed to believe that Steve Kerr is an all-time great coach?

Win a title without Steph Curry. I dare you.

Stan Van Gundy, a thirteen-year NBA head coach who led the Orlando Magic to the NBA Finals in 2009. He is thirtieth all time in wins by an NBA head coach. His career winning percentage is fiftieth, which puts him ahead of Brad Stevens, Don Nelson, Larry Brown, Mike D'Antoni, and Red Holzman.

I HAVE HEARD THIS ARGUMENT FOR YEARS—THAT X coach only wins because he or she has great talent. My first thought is, Well, duh. No coach wins without great talent. I understand that Phil Jackson had Jordan and Pippen and O'Neal and Bryant. Name me the championship team that didn't have great talent.

Popovich had Tim Duncan, Tony Parker, and Manu Ginobili. The Heat won back-to-back titles with LeBron James, Dwyane Wade, and Chris Bosh. The '80s Lakers won with Kareem Abdul-Jabbar, Magic Johnson, and James Worthy. The '80s Celtics won with Larry Bird, Kevin McHale, and Robert Parish. Red Auerbach was probably the first NBA coach to gain acclaim and besides Bill Russell and Bob Cousy he had several other Hall of Famers. Great players are a necessity for winning championships. Everyone knows this—even Stugotz!

I would ask Stugotz this, though. Has he ever considered whether or not he'd be any good at radio without a great co-host like Dan Le Batard? I know I'm not the only one who doesn't listen when Dan is out.

There are no geniuses in coaching. Geniuses make medical and scientific breakthroughs and invent things that change the course of history. Geniuses create great art or find different ways of thinking about the world. Geniuses don't coach basketball. The media label coaches like Gregg Popovich, Steve Kerr, Pat Riley, Bill Belichick, etc. as geniuses, then turn around and tear them down when they lose, inevitably because their star players are hurt, traded, leave, or retire.

However, the fact that there are no coaching geniuses does not mean that coaching doesn't matter nor that anyone could win championships with great players. Winning it all is hard even with the best of rosters. First, the competition is stiff. Think of Jackson's Bulls—they had to beat John Stockton and Karl Malone and Gary Payton and Shawn Kemp. Kerr's Warriors had to beat a team led by one of the greatest players of all time in LeBron James three times. Second, to win multiple championships a coach must keep his team focused and motivated. Any letdown will lead to falling short.

Finally, with everyone targeting these championship teams, great opposing coaches come up with different strategies, and coaches like Jackson and Kerr must be able to adjust, to find answers to everything thrown at them. Maximizing their talent year after year to get their teams across the finish line is a difficult challenge, and both Jackson and Kerr have done it multiple times, and they deserve all of the acclaim they have gotten.

33

WORST IN SHO-HEI

ALL THE SO-CALLED GREAT JAPANESE BASEBALL PLAYERS WHO come over to Major League Baseball eventually get remembered for one thing. Hideo Nomo is remembered for his prolonged windup. Daisuke Matsuzaka is remembered for his Gyro Ball that didn't work in the big leagues. Hideki Irabu is remembered for being fat. Hideki Matsui is remembered for his extensive porn collection. Go ahead. Look it up. I'll wait. Kind of amazing, right? Yu Darvish is remembered for tipping his pitches against the Astros in the 2017 World Series, although there may have been some trash can banging during one of those starts. Ichiro Suzuki is remembered for being one of the best hitters ever. And

Shohei Ohtani will be remembered for ~~having his translator take the fall for a massive gambling debt~~ signing the worst contract in professional sports.

Ohtani began his major league career with the Los Angeles Angels in 2018. That first contract was fine, even though the hype for Ohtani was through the roof. He was billed as the modern-day Babe Ruth because he was supposedly not only a slugger at the plate, but also a starting pitcher with great stuff. As it turned out, Ohtani was just as overrated as the Colossus of Clout.

After starting just ten games in his rookie season, Ohtani blew out his arm and was forced to undergo Tommy John surgery in the offseason. His recovery meant that he couldn't pitch for the entirety of the following season. He couldn't play the field, either, but he could still bat, so he spent his second season as the Angels' designated hitter. Ohtani—again, someone who was sold to us as a slugger—hit just eighteen homers and drove in only sixty-two runs.

Over the next three seasons, Ohtani never drove in more than a hundred runs, won more than ten games only once, and never got the Angels within twelve games of a playoff berth. The MLB voters decided that Ohtani was the MVP of the American League in two of those three seasons, but I have rescinded those awards because the Angels didn't even sniff the postseason. And let me remind you that Major League Baseball added a third wild card spot in each league in 2022, which meant that the top six teams in the AL and the top six teams in the NL made the playoffs. Shohei Ohtani's Angels didn't finish within twelve games of the sixth-place team in the American League in either season.

Ohtani didn't join an Angels team full of losers, either. When Ohtani joined the club, the Angels had two of the greatest players of this generation in Mike Trout and Albert Pujols. Both were listed as Top 30 players in the history of the sport by ESPN in 2022. The Angels lineup also included a pair of four-time All-Stars in Ian Kinsler and Justin Upton, as well as Andrelton Simmons, who finished eighth in MVP voting the year before. You would think that adding a can't-miss Japanese slugger would elevate them to the top of the American League. You would be sadly mistaken, though.

The Angels went 80–82 the year before Ohtani showed up. In his rookie season they went 80–82 again. He literally added nothing to the team. OK. Nothing. In his next four seasons with the Angels, the team never finished with a winning record. They never even won eighty games again. They got worse with Ohtani on the team.

After the 2023 season, in which the Angels finished sixteen games out of the third wild card spot, Ohtani was a free agent. In December he signed a ten-year, $700 million contract with the Los Angeles Dodgers. It was the largest contract in the history of professional sports.

And also the worst.

First and foremost, Shohei Ohtani went to a team that didn't need him. Shohei, the Kevin Durant is strong in you. I mean, let's be honest. The Dodgers won a hundred or more games in three straight seasons before signing Ohtani. The only reason they hadn't won the World Series was because they had Clayton Kershaw getting lit up like a Christmas tree every October.

As for the contract, Ohtani is not worth $700 million. I'm not certain any player is worth $700 million, but I am certain that

Ohtani isn't. At the time of the contract Ohtani was twenty-nine years old, so the Dodgers will be paying him top-of-the-market money as he declines. It's akin to the ten-year deal that the Angels gave Albert Pujols in 2012 except it's worth three times as much. The only thing Pujols ever led the league in with Anaheim was grounding into double plays.

If you want to argue that Ohtani got the massive contract because he's a great hitter and he's a great pitcher, fine, but that argument is fragile. Just like Ohtani's pitching elbow. In August 2023, Ohtani tore the UCL in his right elbow, the same injury that required Tommy John surgery in 2018. The Dodgers signed him knowing that he wouldn't be able to pitch in his first season with the team. Now that he's had two major surgeries on his elbow, he might never pitch again. And if he does pitch, he may not be the same. The list of pitchers to make the All-Star Game after a second UCL reconstruction is short. In fact, it only has one name on it: Nathan Eovaldi.

If Ohtani never pitches again, which is a real concern, the Dodgers will have signed a twenty-nine-year-old who is past his prime and who never drove in more than a hundred runs during his prime to a contract worth $700 million. Ohtani is going to get worse at the plate. No one, other than most of the sport that was juicing in the '90s, gets better as they enter their thirties. He's never driven in more than a hundred runs, so over the course of the contract, Ohtani is likely going to earn more than a million dollars for every run he drives in. Think about that.

The Dodgers offered $700 million for the idea of what Ohtani could be. Not for what he actually is. They'll end up paying a king's ransom for someone who's a myth. A folk hero. Ohtani is more Sidd Finch than he is Babe Ruth.

As bad as the contract was for the Dodgers, Ohtani made it even worse for himself. It seems almost impossible to screw up when you're being paid $700 million, but Shohei found a way.

Ohtani reportedly approached the Dodgers with the idea of deferring 97 percent of the money owed to him. So, the Dodgers will pay him $2 million in each of the ten seasons of the contract, which runs through 2033. Then they'll owe him $68 million, interest-free, in each of the ten years after that, through 2043. It's just a staggeringly dumb decision. Ohtani should take that money as quickly as he can get his paws on it and let it work for him. Time is money. As someone who used to sling munis to guys named Murray, I would know. Conservatively speaking, Ohtani is costing himself nearly $200 million by deferring the money interest-free.

I think the MLB Players Association should have stepped in and stopped this from happening. Not because it's hurting Ohtani. But because it's hurting the legacy of Bobby Bonilla. Bobby Bo gets about $1.2 million every July 1 from the New York Mets as part of a contract buyout in 2000. Only the Mets could have turned the $5.9 million they owed him into the nearly $30 million he will end up getting. Either way, when Bobby Bo gets the last check for $1.2 million in 2035, Shohei Ohtani will get his second deferred payment of $68 million. Bobby Bonilla Day will become Shohei Ohtani Day, and I don't like it one bit. The sports world revels in celebrating the Mets' incompetence every July. Don't take that away from us. As Mets fans, that's all we have.

And, Shohei, just so we're clear, any World Series won with the Dodgers over the course of this ridiculous contract will not count in this record book.

David Samson, former Marlins team president and host of *Nothing Personal with David Samson*

THERE IS NO WORSE FEELING THAN GETTING A MISSED call from Stugotz. In the two decades that I have known him, he has only called me when he needs something. This particular phone call was on a subject that I feared would cross my desk at some point. I learned that he was "writing" a book in what I had hoped would be a bit on *The Dan Le Batard Show with Stugotz*. It turns out that Stugotz wanted me to help perpetuate the rumor that he is both a journalist and an informed media personality.

It certainly tracks that he would rely on others to write his book for him. It is hard to say that Stugotz has incorrect takes without first understanding what a take is. A take is an opinion, and opinions can never be wrong, only facts. I have hesitated to criticize anyone for a take, because I choose to believe that a person willing to give his opinion should always be allowed to do so. Issues arise when takes are based on misinformation or simple laziness. The best part about Stugotz's thinking that Shohei Ohtani's contract is the worst contract of all time is that his use of hyperbole is neither factual nor opinionated. It is simple page filler.

Where is the conversation about net present value or the discount rate or a basic understanding of a contract not seen through the lens of a supposed Mets fan (who truly couldn't name four members of the current Mets team). If Stugotz thinks I am going to write a paragraph either agreeing or disagreeing with his take, he is sorely mistaken. If Stugotz thinks I am going to take the time to develop a top five list of contracts that are worse than Shohei Ohtani's and use this book as a platform to release said top five, he is again sorely mistaken.

Getting through an argument, either oral or written, requires the two combatants to be passionate, opinionated, thoughtful, articulate, intelligent, hardworking, and willing to believe that they may be wrong. Stugotz checks zero of the boxes. The only thing worse than Shohei's contract is Stugotz's. The only thing more certain than Shohei's not generating sufficient revenue to guarantee a return for the Dodgers is Meadowlark's feeling the same way about Stugotz.

One should also note that there is no direct correlation with the many press conferences the Dodgers have had announcing all the new corporate partnerships with Japanese companies. No matter how many times Shohei wins Player of the Week or MVP, the Dodgers will never disclose the true return on investment. However, none of these facts indicate that his contract is the worst ever. It simply indicates that the Dodgers are able to spend money in amounts that make twenty-eight other Major League Baseball teams jealous. They say that money can't buy happiness or World Series rings. Stugotz believes that money, heaters, and general malaise are the tickets to his success. I guess on all these matters, we will have to #waittosee.

34

THE PHILLY SPECIAL

IF YOU WERE TO GOOGLE WHO THE MVP OF SUPER BOWL LII was, the search results would tell you that it was Nick Foles. But that Google search, like many a Wikipedia entry, is wrong.

No one, and I mean no one, has ever been set up to succeed more than Nick Foles was in 2017. Think about what he had going for him when he was called into action.

Carson Wentz had led the Philadelphia Eagles to an 11–2 record. They had earned the #1 seed in the NFC. They had secured home-field advantage throughout the playoffs. Wentz was having an MVP-type season before tearing his ACL in Week 14. He was so good that he still finished third in the MVP voting.

That was a talented Eagles team, too. They had one of the best offensive lines we've ever seen. I mean, they were littered with All-Pros and Pro Bowlers up front on both sides of the ball. They had a Pro Bowl security blanket in Zach Ertz for Foles to throw to. And they had a top five defense anchored by Pro Bowl safety Malcolm Jenkins.

Not only that, but you couldn't dream up a better offensive coaching staff to support Foles. Now, as I've correctly stated numerous times throughout this book, coaching does not matter much when you have Michael Jordan and Scottie Pippen or Kobe Bryant and Shaquille O'Neal. But when a backup quarterback enters the game, having coaches who've been in the same situation before can do a world of good. And that's what Nick Foles had with the Eagles.

Philadelphia's head coach was Doug Pederson, who made a career backing up legends like Dan Marino and Brett Favre. Philly's offensive coordinator was Frank Reich, who backed up Hall of Famer Jim Kelly in Buffalo and engineered the greatest comeback in playoff history.

Trust me when I tell you that Jolly Old Saint Nick Foles was no hero. He did not save the day. He was nothing more than a caretaker. He was a co-pilot on a cross-country flight who monitored the autopilot system while the captain was taking a piss. It would have been hard for him not to succeed in that environment.

Super Bowl MVP? Please. I don't want to hear about it. There is no Super Bowl if Carson Wentz doesn't get the team off to an 11–2 start.

Listen, I will not live in a world where Nick Foles has one more Super Bowl ring than Dan Marino. I refuse to. Foles came in and played a handful of regular-season games that didn't actually matter because Wentz had already locked up the #1 seed and home-field advantage. All Foles had to do was keep everything moving forward. He kept the boat afloat. That's essentially what he did. Good for you, Nick Foles. You kept things moving forward. You didn't screw things up. But you don't get a ring simply for not sinking the ship.

In the playoffs the Eagles squeaked by a 10–6 Falcons team in the divisional round thanks to a goal-line stand by their defense. Foles and the offense mustered only fifteen points. In the NFC Championship Game, Foles outgunned Case Keenum and the Vikings, who had no business being in that game after the refs completely missed the worst pass interference in the history of the playoffs against the Saints. Congrats on besting an undrafted quarterback who started ten games in a season just twice in his career. I mean, seriously. Talk about a cakewalk to the Super Bowl.

Listen up, Foles. You had home-field advantage. One of the greatest offensive lines we've ever seen. All you had to do was win a couple of home playoff games, which any decent quarterback can do. Trent Dilfer did it. Rex Grossman won a few. Even Brock Osweiler won a home playoff game, so I don't want to hear about it, OK? And then you played in the Super Bowl, Philly Special, and all of a sudden you're some kind of legend. A legend you are not.

I've got news for you, Nick Foles. You don't even have a ring. Carson Wentz is the only quarterback on that Philadelphia Eagles team who deserved one. Your reward for being gifted the opportunity to play in the Super Bowl is the $88 million the Jaguars gave you to go 0–4 as a starter in 2019.

35

REIGN OVER ME

THE DENVER NUGGETS WON THE NBA CHAMPIONSHIP IN JUNE 2023 and right away the murmuring began. Is this the beginning of a dynasty? The think pieces were written: "Inside the Denver Nuggets' Plan to Build a Dynasty."

A dynasty? It was Denver's first-ever trip to the NBA Finals!

They followed up their championship season by getting bounced in the second round by the Minnesota Timberwolves. A dynasty it was not.

The University of Georgia won back-to-back college football championships in 2021 and 2022. In the immediate aftermath

ESPN ran a story with the headline: "Georgia Dynasty Is Just Beginning."

They didn't even make it to the College Football Playoff the following year.

Can we all just slow down and take a breath?

It took overtime for the Kansas City Chiefs to beat the San Francisco 49ers in Super Bowl LVIII. That title gave Patrick Mahomes, Travis Kelce, and dem boys three rings in a five-year stretch. They just barely qualified for dynasty status. Had they lost, I would not have considered them a dynasty. In fact, I had this whole chapter written explaining why they weren't a dynasty, but now they are. *Just barely.*

Why is everyone in sports media so quick to call a good team a dynasty? Do you get credit for being the first to anoint a team as a dynasty or something? Are there kickbacks for granting dynasty status? Trust me, if there were I would have been calling the Nuggets a dynasty when they had Kiki VanDeWeghe and the Chiefs a dynasty when they had Alex Smith. Here's the thing about dynasties. They are not given. They're earned. You can't go around proclaiming teams as dynasties. They show themselves to *you,* not the other way around. The real dynasties are not questioned. They are obvious. That's actually the first rule about dynasties. If there's any doubt, then it's not a dynasty.

Here's a dynasty—the Chicago Bulls in the 1990s. Eight straight titles. An eight-peat. MJ. Pippen. Horace Grant for a few of them, Rodman for a few, and Toni Kukoč for some as well. That's a dynasty.

The Dallas Cowboys in the early '90s. Three Super Bowls in four years. Troy Aikman. Emmitt Smith. Michael Irvin. Jimmy Johnson. Jay Novacek. Daryl "Moose" Johnston. Charles Haley.

Leon Lett. Deion Sanders—Prime Time—for one of them. They dominated those Buffalo Bills teams with Jim Kelly and Thurman Thomas. Dynasty.

The early 1980s New York Islanders in hockey. They won four consecutive Stanley Cups. Made it to five. Hockey actually had three dynasties in a row from 1976 to 1990. First it was the Montreal Canadiens, who won the Stanley Cup four years in a row. Then it was the Islanders for four straight years. And then the Edmonton Oilers, who won five in seven years with Wayne Gretzky—The Great One, and Mark Messier—The Messiah. Dynasty dynasty dynasty.

The last dynasty we had in baseball was the late-'90s New York Yankees, which won the World Series four times in a five-year stretch. They had the core four of Derek Jeter, Bernie Williams, Jorge Posada, and Mariano Rivera. Winning four in five years in a sport as random as baseball leaves no doubt. That was a dynasty.

What about the Bruce Bochy Giants of 2010–14, which won the World Series three times in five years? Do they get dynasty status? No. That was not a dynasty. I honestly don't remember a single one of those teams. I'm told they beat the Rangers, Royals, and Tigers in those World Series, but I have no memory of them. Now, I know I've done a lot of drugs in my life, but I still remember the late-'90s Yankees. There isn't a brain cell with any knowledge about this Giants run. Rule number two—in order to be a dynasty you have to be memorable, and there was nothing memorable about that stretch for the Giants. I'm not telling my grandkids about Buster Posey. Sorry. I'm just not.

You want a memorable dynasty? How about the Bill Walsh San Francisco 49ers of the '80s? They won four Super Bowls in the decade and revolutionized offense in the NFL. They had some of the greatest players of all time in Jerry Rice and Joe Montana, as well as one of the most iconic plays in all of sports. The Catch. Montana to Dwight Clark in the back of the end zone to beat the Cowboys in the NFC title game back in 1981. That was a dynasty. Now, you don't necessarily have to have one of the most famous sports plays ever to be a dynasty, but it helps.

Nick Saban's time at Alabama was certainly a dynasty. From 2009 to 2020 the Crimson Tide won the national championship six times. That's half of them. Saban's teams were memorable for their dominant defenses, often mediocre quarterback play by the likes of Greg McElroy and A. J. McCarron, and elite offensive weapons (Mark Ingram, Julio Jones, Derrick Henry, Jerry Jeudy, and DeVonta Smith, to name a few). They were in the conversation every single year. Another part of being a dynasty is staying relevant and in the upper echelon of your respective sport. Saban did that with the Tide. That's rule number three. You have to be in the championship conversation for the majority of your run. You can't win a title, miss the playoffs for two years, win another title, and call yourself a dynasty.

Like the Ben Roethlisberger Pittsburgh Steelers. Sure, they won two Super Bowls in four years, but they were not a dynasty. They won it all in 2005 and 2008, but they missed the playoffs in 2006 and lost in the first round in 2007. They made a splash, but they didn't stay in the pool long enough. Not a dynasty.

The Steel Curtain Steelers of the 1970s? That was a dynasty. They had great players like Terry Bradshaw, Franco Harris, Mean Joe Greene, and Lynn Swann. They also had one of the most famous plays in the history of sports with "The Immaculate Reception." Their defense had a cool nickname. And they won four Super Bowls in a six-year stretch. They went back-to-back twice.

Dabo Swinney won two titles in three years at Clemson. They bested Nick Saban's Alabama teams in both championship games they won. They went to four CFP Championship Games in five years. Not a dynasty. Sorry. Part of being a dynasty is winning titles back-to-back. There is something about going from the hunter to the hunted that some teams don't quite have. A lot of teams get content after they win a title and can't get themselves as motivated to win another one. All the great dynasties in sports relish the opportunity to defend their title. Oftentimes they are hungrier to win the second one. Winning a title and then staying on the mountaintop the following year is a statement. Fending off all the other challengers for a full year is a requirement for a team to be considered a dynasty. That's rule number four. You have to go back-to-back.

The Chicago Blackhawks won the Stanley Cup in 2010, 2013, and 2015. A great run by Joel Quenneville and company, but it wasn't a dynasty.

Urban Meyer won two national championships in three years at Florida with an iconic player in Tim Tebow, but that wasn't a dynasty either.

The Miami Heat with LeBron James, Dwyane Wade, and Chris Bosh check a lot of the boxes. They went to the Finals four straight times and won back-to-back titles in 2011 and 2012. They were relevant. They were memorable. The Ray Allen shot to send Game 6 of the 2012 Finals into overtime might be the greatest shot in the history of basketball. But they weren't a dynasty.

The Toronto Blue Jays won back-to-back World Series in 1992 and 1993. They had some all-time greats on those teams. Paul Molitor. Rickey Henderson. Roberto Alomar. Joe Carter's walk-off home run to win the 1993 World Series is one of the most famous moments in the annals of baseball. They weren't a dynasty either.

Two is not enough. That's the fifth and final rule. You have to win more than two titles to be considered a dynasty. A lot of teams win two. Kobe and Pau Gasol won two with the Lakers. Not a dynasty. Isiah Thomas and the Pistons won two. Not a dynasty. The Pittsburgh Penguins and Tampa Bay Lightning have both recently won two in a row. Neither of those were dynasties. John Elway won two Super Bowls with the Broncos at the end of his career. Not a dynasty.

FIVE RULES TO BE CONSIDERED A DYNASTY IN SPORTS

1. It must be obvious. If there's any doubt, then it's not a dynasty.
2. You have to be memorable.
3. You have to stay in the championship mix.
4. You have to win back-to-back titles.
5. You have to win more than two titles.

So let's slow down with this talk of a dynasty for the Denver Nuggets and every other team with a great player that wins one championship. They have a long way to go before they get to dynasty status. They've reached the mountaintop once. Do it again. And then do it one more time and then maybe we can talk dynasty.

Seriously, that's why I always say, "Do it on the road. Do it in the playoffs. Do it in the championship game. And then do it again." That is how you build a legacy in sports.

I can't believe it took me until the last chapter of the book to discover my own thesis.

Actually, I can believe that.

ACKNOWLEDGMENTS

FIRST AND FOREMOST, THANK YOU TO THE TWENTY FORMER athletes, journalists, and members of the sports media who took the time to entertain the arguments we made in this book before strongly rebutting them. As we told them all, it wouldn't be a Stugotz project without asking some smart, famous friends to do some of the work.

This book does not happen without Mike Schur. Thank you for your support, your advice, and, most important, for introducing us to the best literary agent in the world, Richard Abate. Richard, the counsel and direction that you provided were invaluable.

A big thanks to our editor, Ben Greenberg, for his belief in the vision of this book. After our first meeting we knew that he was the right person for the job, and he proved us right every step of the way with his passion, kindness, and undeniable talent. Thank you to Ayelet Durantt, Leila Tejani, Greg Kubie, Alison Rich, and the rest of the team at Random House for bringing enthusiasm and ideas to every meeting. It was a joy working with you all.

Thank you to Angel Resto, whose artwork beautifully complements every chapter.

Thanks to Dan Le Batard and everyone at Meadowlark Media for intuitively knowing the best ways to discuss this endeavor on the air. A special shout-out to JuJu Gotti for his tireless work promoting the book on social media and to Mike Fuentes for delivering important metrics in a timely manner.

Now we'd like to thank some people separately.

Stugotz: I'd like to thank my wife and kids for putting up with me during this process and, really, for just putting up with me in general. Thank you to Dan Stanczyk for bringing this book to life. His relentless work ethic and belief in me and this project are the only reasons this book got done. And, of course, a big thanks to Kevin Durant for not staying in Oklahoma City.

Stanczyk: I'd like to thank my college professor Fran Silverman for helping me realize that I had a knack for writing. Her kindness and encouragement gave me the confidence to pursue future projects, including this one.

Thank you to my amazing wife, Jenna, and our wonderful kids for all their love and support. I lost track of the number of times Jenna had to tend to the kids while also making dinner (after a full day of work and a long commute) as Stugotz and I were on the phone talking about Ray Bourque, Joe Mauer, or whatever we needed to do before our next meeting or deadline.

ABOUT THE AUTHORS

Jon "Stugotz" Weiner is a sports talk host who has developed an army of supporters by embodying the voice of the fan. Stugotz started 790 The Ticket (WAXY) in South Florida and has served as the co-host of *The Dan Le Batard Show with Stugotz* for twenty years (syndicated nationally on ESPN Radio from 2014 to 2021). He also hosts the popular podcasts *STUpodity* and *God Bless Football*. He received his BA in English from Clark University. He lives in Parkland, Florida, with his wife, Abby, and their twin daughters.

Dan Stanczyk is a sports-talk-radio-turned-podcast producer who has worked with current and former athletes, reporters, and analysts to craft compelling arguments across multiple platforms. Stanczyk has spearheaded the content creation for *The Herd with Colin Cowherd, Mike & Mike, Golic and Wingo, STUpodity, The Lowe Post, The Woj Pod, Cinephile with Adnan Virk, The Mina Kimes Show featuring Lenny, That's What She Said with Sarah Spain, The Right Time with Bomani Jones,* and many other shows. He received his BA in communications from Fairfield University. He lives in Stratford, Connecticut, with his wife, Jenna, and their children.

stugotzbook.com

X: @lebatardshow, @stugotz790, @DanStanczyk

Instagram: @lebatardshow,
@stugotz790, @danstanczyk

ABOUT THE TYPE

This book was set in Bulmer, a typeface designed in the late eighteenth century by the London type cutter William Martin (1757–1830). The typeface was created especially for the Shakespeare Press, directed by William Bulmer (1757–1830)—hence the font's name. Bulmer is considered to be a transitional typeface, containing characteristics of old-style and modern designs. It is recognized for its elegantly proportioned letters, with their long ascenders and descenders.